*AICPA Audit Guide*

# SERVICE ORGANIZATIONS: APPLYING SAS NO. 70, AS AMENDED

## With Conforming Changes as of May 1, 2005

This edition of the AICPA Audit and Accounting Guide *Service Organizations: Applying SAS No. 70, as Amended,* which was originally issued in 2002, has been modified by the AICPA staff to include certain changes necessary because of the issuance of authoritative pronouncements since the Guide was originally issued (see page iv). The changes made for the current year are identified in a schedule in Appendix H of the Guide. The changes do *not* include all those that might be considered necessary if the Guide were subjected to a comprehensive review and revision.

AMERICAN INSTITUTE OF CERTIFIED PUBLIC ACCOUNTANTS

AICPA

# Notice to Readers

This AICPA Audit Guide was prepared by the AICPA SAS No. 70 Task Force to assist auditors in applying generally accepted auditing standards in audits of financial statements of entities that use service organizations and in service auditors' engagements. The AICPA's Auditing Standards Board has found the descriptions of auditing standards, procedures, and practices in this Audit Guide to be consistent with existing standards covered by Rule 202 and 203 of the AICPA Code of Professional Conduct.

This AICPA Audit Guide, which contains auditing guidance, is an interpretive publication pursuant to SAS No. 95, *Generally Accepted Auditing Standards*. Interpretive publications are recommendations on the application of SASs in specific circumstances, including engagements for entities in specialized industries. Interpretive publications are issued under the authority of the Auditing Standards Board. The members of the Auditing Standards Board have found this Guide to be consistent with existing SASs.

The auditor should be aware of and consider interpretive publications applicable to his or her audit. If the auditor does not apply the auditing guidance included in an applicable interpretive publication, the auditor should be prepared to explain how he or she complied with the SAS provisions addressed by such auditing guidance.

## Public Accounting Firms Registered With the PCAOB

Subject to the Securities and Exchange Commission (Commission) oversight, Section 103 of the Sarbanes-Oxley Act (Act) authorizes the Public Company Accounting Oversight Board (PCAOB) to establish auditing and related attestation, quality control, ethics, and independence standards to be used by registered public accounting firms in the preparation and issuance of audit reports as required by the Act or the rules of the Commission. Accordingly, public accounting firms registered with the PCAOB are required to adhere to all PCAOB standards in the audits of issuers, as defined by the Act, and other entities when prescribed by the rules of the Commission.

John A. Fogarty, *Chair*
Auditing Standards Board

## SAS No. 70 Task Force

George H. Tucker, *Chair*          Patrick H. Scott
Susan E. Kenney                    Thomas Wallace
Andrew E. Nolan

## AICPA Staff

Charles E. Landes                  Judith M. Sherinsky
*Vice President*                   *Technical Manager*
*Professional Standards and Services*    *Audit and Attest Standards*

Linda C. Delahanty
*Technical Manager*
*Accounting and Auditing Publications*

The Auditing Standards Board is grateful to Michael Davidson for his technical assistance with this document.

This edition of the Guide has been modified by the AICPA staff to include certain changes necessary due to the issuance of authoritative pronouncements since the Guide was originally issued. Relevant auditing guidance contained in official pronouncements through May 1, 2005 have been considered in the development of this edition of the Guide. This includes relevant guidance issued up to and including the following:

- SAS No. 101, *Auditing Fair Value Measurements and Disclosures*
- SOP 04-1, *Auditing the Statement of Social Insurance*
- SSAE No. 12, *Amendment to Statement on Standards for Attestation Engagements No. 10*, Attestation Standards: Revision and Recodification
- PCAOB Auditing Standard No. 3, *Audit Documentation*

Users of this Guide should consider pronouncements issued subsequent to those listed above to determine their effect on entities covered by this Guide.

This edition of the AICPA Audit Guide *Service Organizations: Applying SAS No. 70, as Amended*, which was originally issued in April 2002, has been modified by the AICPA staff to include certain changes necessary because of the issuance of authoritative pronouncements since the Guide was originally issued. The changes made are identified in a schedule in Appendix H of the Guide. The changes do not include all those that might be considered necessary if the Guide were subjected to a comprehensive review and revision.

# Preface

This Audit Guide *Service Organizations: Applying SAS No. 70, as Amended* is designed to provide guidance to service auditors engaged to issue reports on a service organization's controls that may be part of a user organization's information system in the context of an audit of financial statements. It also provides guidance to user auditors engaged to audit the financial statements of entities that use service organizations. Guidance on performing service auditors' engagements and using service auditors' reports in audits of financial statements is provided in Statement on Auditing Standards (SAS) No. 70, *Service Organizations*.

This Guide was initially issued as an Auditing Procedure Study titled *Implementing SAS No. 70, Reports on the Processing of Transactions by Service Organizations*. In 1998, it was reissued as an Auditing Practice Release and was revised to incorporate the guidance in SAS No. 78, *Consideration of Internal Control in a Financial Statement Audit: An Amendment to SAS No. 55*. SAS No. 78 revises the definition and description of internal control contained in SAS No. 55, *Consideration of Internal Control in a Financial Statement Audit*, to recognize the definition and description contained in *Internal Control—Integrated Framework*, published by the Committee of Sponsoring Organizations of the Treadway Commission. This version of the document is an Audit Guide. In April 2002, it was revised to reflect the issuance of SAS No. 88, *Service Organizations and Reporting on Consistency*, which clarifies the applicability of SAS No. 70, as amended. It also reflected the paragraph renumbering in SAS No. 94, *The Effect of Information Technology on the Auditor's Consideration of Internal Control in a Financial Statement Audit*. SAS No. 94 amends SAS No. 55 to provide guidance to auditors about the effect of information technology on internal control, and on the auditor's understanding of internal control and assessment of control risk. Throughout this Guide, SAS No. 55, as amended by SAS No. 78 and SAS No. 94, is referred to as SAS No. 55, as amended, and SAS No. 70, as amended by SAS No. 78, No. 88, and No. 98, *Omnibus Statement on Auditing Standards—2002* is referred to as SAS No. 70, as amended.

This Audit Guide is part of a series issued by the AICPA and was drafted by the SAS No. 70 Task Force of the Auditing Standards Board.

## Auditing Guidance Included in this Guide and References to AICPA and PCAOB Professional Standards

This Guide presents auditing guidance to help you implement auditing standards included in both AICPA professional standards ("GAAS") and in PCAOB professional standards. In referring to AICPA professional standards, this Guide cites the applicable sections of the AICPA *Professional Standards* publication. In referring to PCAOB standards, this Guide cites the applicable sections of the AICPA's publication titled *PCAOB Standards and Related Rules*. In those cases in which the auditing standards of the AICPA and those of the PCAOB are the same, this Guide cites the applicable section of the AICPA *Professional Standards* publication only.

## Substantial Changes to Audit Process Proposed

The AICPA's Auditing Standards Board (ASB) issued an exposure draft proposing seven new Statements on Auditing Standards (SASs) relating to the auditor's risk assessment process. The ASB believes that the requirements and guidance provided in the proposed SASs, if adopted, would result in a substantial change in audit practice and in more effective audits. The primary objective of the proposed SASs is to enhance auditors' application of the audit risk model in practice by requiring:

- A more in-depth understanding of the entity and its environment, including its internal control, to identify the risks of material misstatement in the financial statements and what the entity is doing to mitigate them.

- A more rigorous assessment of the risks of material misstatement of the financial statements based on that understanding.

- Improved linkage between the assessed risks and the nature, timing and extent of audit procedures performed in response to those risks.

The exposure draft consists of the following proposed SASs:

- *Amendment to Statement on Auditing Standards No. 95, Generally Accepted Auditing Standards*

- *Audit Evidence*

- *Audit Risk and Materiality in Conducting an Audit*

- *Planning and Supervision*

- *Understanding the Entity and Its Environment and Assessing the Risks of Material Misstatement*

- *Performing Audit Procedures in Response to Assessed Risks and Evaluating the Audit Evidence Obtained*

- *Amendment to Statement on Auditing Standards No. 39, Audit Sampling*

The proposed SASs establish standards and provide guidance concerning the auditor's assessment of the risks of material misstatement in a financial statement audit, and the design and performance of audit procedures whose nature, timing, and extent are responsive to the assessed risks. Additionally, the proposed SASs establish standards and provide guidance on planning and supervision, the nature of audit evidence, and evaluating whether the audit evidence obtained affords a reasonable basis for an opinion regarding the financial statements under audit.

The proposed standards are expected to be issued as final standards at the end of 2005. Readers can access the proposed standards at AICPA Online (www.aicpa.org) and should be alert to future progress on this project.

## Applicability of Requirements of the Sarbanes-Oxley Act of 2002, Related Securities and Exchange Commission Regulations, and Standards of the Public Company Accounting Oversight Board

Publicly-held companies and other "issuers" (see definition below) are subject to the provisions of the Sarbanes-Oxley Act of 2002 (Act) and related Securities and Exchange Commission (SEC) regulations implementing the Act. Their outside auditors are also subject to the provisions of the Act and to the rules and standards issued by the Public Company Accounting Oversight Board (PCAOB).

Presented below is a summary of certain key areas addressed by the Act, the SEC, and the PCAOB that are particularly relevant to the preparation and issuance of an issuer's financial statements and the preparation and issuance of an audit report on those financial statements. However, the provisions of the Act, the regulations of the SEC, and the rules and standards of the PCAOB are numerous and are not all addressed in this section or in this Guide. Issuers and their auditors should understand the provisions of the Act, the SEC regulations implementing the Act, and the rules and standards of the PCAOB, as applicable to their circumstances.

*Definition of an Issuer*

The Act states that the term "issuer" means an issuer (as defined in section 3 of the Securities Exchange Act of 1934 (15 U.S.C. 78c)), the securities of which are registered under section 12 of that Act (15 U.S.C. 78l), or that is required to file reports under section 15(d) (15 U.S.C. 78o(d)), or that files or has filed a registration statement that has not yet become effective under the Securities Act of 1933 (15 U.S.C. 77a et seq.), and that it has not withdrawn.

Issuers, as defined by the Act, and other entities when prescribed by the rules of the SEC (collectively referred to in this Guide as "issuers" or "issuer") and their public accounting firms (who must be registered with the PCAOB) are subject to the provisions of the Act, implementing SEC regulations, and the rules and standards of the PCAOB, as appropriate.

Non-issuers are those entities not subject to the Act or the rules of the SEC.

# Guidance for Issuers

## Management Assessment of Internal Control

As directed by Section 404 of the Act, the SEC adopted final rules requiring companies subject to the reporting requirements of the Securities Exchange Act of 1934, other than registered investment companies and certain other entities, to include in their annual reports a report of management on the company's internal control over financial reporting. See the SEC web site at www.sec.gov/rules/final/33-8238.htm for the full text of the regulation.

Companies that are "accelerated filers," as defined in Exchange Act Rule 12b-2, are required to comply with these rules for fiscal years ending on or after November 15, 2004. "Non-accelerated filers" and foreign private issuers filing their annual reports on Form 20-F or 40-F must begin to comply with the rules for the first fiscal year ending on or after July 15, 2006. See the SEC web site at www.sec.gov/rules/final/33-8545.htm for further information.

The SEC rules clarify that management's assessment and report is limited to *internal control over financial reporting*. The SEC's definition of internal control encompasses the Committee of Sponsoring Organizations of the Treadway Commission (COSO) definition but the SEC does not mandate that the entity use COSO as its criteria for judging effectiveness.

Under the SEC rules, the company's annual 10-K must include:

1. Management's Annual Report on Internal Control Over Financial Reporting
2. Attestation Report of the Registered Public Accounting Firm
3. Changes in Internal Control Over Financial Reporting

The SEC rules also require management to evaluate any change in the entity's internal control that occurred during a fiscal quarter and that has materially affected, or is reasonably likely to materially affect, the entity's internal control over financial reporting.

## Audit Committees and Corporate Governance

Section 301 of the Act establishes requirements related to the makeup and the responsibilities of an issuer's audit committee. Among those requirements—

- Each member of the audit committee must be a member of the board of directors of the issuer, and otherwise be independent.
- The audit committee of an issuer is directly responsible for the appointment, compensation, and oversight of the work of any registered public accounting firm employed by that issuer.
- The audit committee shall establish procedures for the "receipt, retention, and treatment of complaints" received by the issuer regarding accounting, internal controls, and auditing.

In April 2003, the SEC adopted a rule to direct the national securities exchanges and national securities associations to prohibit the listing of any security of an issuer that is not in compliance with the audit committee requirements mandated by the Act.

## Disclosure of Audit Committee Financial Expert and Code of Ethics

In January 2003, the SEC adopted amendments requiring issuers, other than registered investment companies, to include two new types of disclosures in their annual reports filed pursuant to the Securities Exchange Act of 1934. These amendments conform to Sections 406 and 407 of the Act and relate to disclosures concerning the audit committee's financial expert and code of ethics relating to the companies' officers. An amendment specifies that these disclosures are only required for annual reports.

## Certification of Disclosure in an Issuer's Quarterly and Annual Reports

Section 302 of the Act requires the Chief Executive Officer (CEO) and Chief Financial Officer (CFO) of each issuer to prepare a statement to accompany the audit report to certify the "appropriateness of the financial statements and disclosures contained in the periodic report, and that those financial statements and disclosures fairly present, in all material respects, the operations and financial condition of the issuer."

In August 2002, the SEC adopted final rules for Certification of Disclosure in Companies' Quarterly and Annual Reports in response to Section 302 of the Act. CEOs and CFOs are now required to certify the financial and other information contained in quarterly and annual reports.

## Improper Influence on Conduct of Audits

Section 303 of the Act makes it unlawful for any officer or director of an issuer to take any action to fraudulently influence, coerce, manipulate, or mislead any auditor engaged in the performance of an audit for the purpose of rendering the financial statements materially misleading. In April 2003, the SEC adopted rules implementing these provisions of the Act.

## Disclosures in Periodic Reports

Section 401(a) of the Act requires that each financial report of an issuer that is required to be prepared in accordance with generally accepted accounting principles (GAAP) shall "reflect all material correcting adjustments . . . that have been identified by a registered accounting firm . . . ." In addition, "each annual and quarterly financial report . . . shall disclose all material off-balance sheet transactions" and "other relationships" with "unconsolidated entities" that may have a material current or future effect on the financial condition of the issuer.

In January 2003, the SEC adopted rules that require disclosure of material off-balance sheet transactions, arrangements, obligations, and other relationships of the issuer with unconsolidated entities or other persons, that may have a material current or future effect on financial condition, changes in financial condition, results of operations, liquidity, capital expenditures, capital resources, or significant components of revenues or expenses. The rules require an issuer to provide an explanation of its off-balance sheet arrangements in a separately captioned subsection of the Management's Discussion and Analysis section of an issuer's disclosure documents.

# Guidance for Auditors

The Act mandates a number of requirements concerning auditors of issuers, including mandatory registration with the PCAOB, the setting of auditing standards, inspections, investigations, disciplinary proceedings, prohibited activities, partner rotation, and reports to audit committees, among others. Auditors of issuers should familiarize themselves with applicable provisions of the Act and the standards of the PCAOB. The PCAOB continues to establish rules and standards implementing provisions of the Act concerning the auditors of issuers.

## Applicability of Generally Accepted Auditing Standards and Public Company Accounting Oversight Board Standards

The Act authorizes the PCAOB to establish auditing and related attestation, quality control, ethics, and independence standards to be used by registered public accounting firms in the preparation and issuance of audit reports for entities subject to the Act or the rules of the SEC. Accordingly, public accounting firms registered with the PCAOB are required to adhere to all PCAOB standards in the audits of "issuers," as defined by the Act, and other entities when prescribed by the rules of the SEC.

For those entities not subject to the Act or the rules of the SEC, the preparation and issuance of audit reports remain governed by GAAS as issued by the ASB.

## Major Existing Differences Between GAAS and PCAOB Standards

The major differences between GAAS and PCAOB standards are described in both Part I of volume one of the AICPA *Professional Standards* and in Part I of the AICPA publication titled, *PCAOB Standards and Related Rules.*

## Auditor Reports to Audit Committees

Section 204 of the Act requires the accounting firm to report to the issuer's audit committee all "critical accounting policies and practices to be used . . . all alternative treatments of financial information within [GAAP] that have been discussed with management ... ramifications of the use of such alternative disclosures and treatments, and the treatment preferred" by the firm..

## Other Requirements

The Act contains requirements in a number of other important areas, and the SEC has issued implementing regulations in certain of those areas as well. For example,

- The Act prohibits auditors from performing certain non-audit or non-attest services. The SEC adopted amendments to its existing requirements regarding auditor independence to enhance the independence of accountants that audit and review financial statements and prepare attestation reports filed with the SEC. This rule conforms the SEC's regulations to Section 208(a) of the Act and, importantly, addresses the performance of non-audit services.

- The Act requires the lead audit or coordinating partner and the reviewing partner to rotate off of the audit every 5 years. (See SEC Releases 33-8183 and 33-8183A for SEC implementing rules.)

- The Act directs the PCAOB to require a second partner review and approval of audit reports (concurring review).

- The Act states that an accounting firm will not be able to provide audit services to an issuer if one of that issuer's top officials (CEO, Controller, CFO, Chief Accounting Officer, etc.) was employed by the firm and worked on the issuer's audit during the previous year.

# Introduction<sup>*</sup>

**I-01** Many entities use outside service organizations to accomplish tasks that affect the entity's financial statements. Service organizations provide services ranging from performing a specific task under the direction of an entity to replacing entire business units or functions of an entity. In recent years, there has been a significant increase in the use of service organizations. Because many of the functions performed by service organizations affect an entity's financial statements, auditors performing audits of financial statements may need to obtain information about those services, the related service organization controls, and their effects on an entity's financial statements.

**I-02** Examples of service organizations that perform functions that may affect other entities' financial statements are bank trust departments that hold and service assets for employee benefit plans or for others, mortgage bankers that service mortgages for others, and application service providers that provide software applications and a technology environment that enables customers to process financial and operational transactions.

**I-03** An auditor may be engaged to issue a report on a service organization's controls for use by user organizations and their auditors. Statement on Auditing Standards (SAS) No. 70, *Service Organizations*, as amended (AICPA, *Professional Standards*, vol. 1, AU sec. 324),[1] provides guidance to an auditor performing (1) an audit of a user organization's financial statements, and (2) procedures at a service organization that will enable the auditor to issue a service auditor's report on a service organization's controls that may be part of user organizations' information systems. Although a service auditor's report may be used by management of a service organization and its user organizations, its primary purpose is to provide information to auditors who audit user organizations' financial statements. The purpose of this Guide is to help auditors of entities that use service organizations (user auditors) and auditors issuing reports on the controls of service organizations (service auditors) implement SAS No. 70, as amended.

**I-04** Publicly-held companies and other "issuers" are subject to the provisions of the Sarbanes-Oxley Act of 2002 (Act) and related Securities and Exchange Commission (SEC) regulations implementing the Act. Their outside auditors are also subject to the provisions of the Act and to the rules and standards issued by the Public Company Accounting Oversight Board (PCAOB). The PCAOB adopted as interim standards, on an initial, transitional basis, the AICPA generally accepted auditing standards in existence on April 16, 2003. In September 2004 certain of these interim standards were amended by PCAOB Release 2004-008, *Conforming Amendments to PCAOB Interim Standards Resulting from the Adoption of PCAOB Auditing Standard No. 2*, "An Audit

---

<sup>*</sup> Refer to the Preface of this Guide for important information about the applicability of the professional standards to audits of issuers and non-issuers (see definitions in the Preface).

[1] The title of Statement on Auditing Standards (SAS) No. 70, *Service Organizations*, as amended (AICPA, *Professional Standards*, vol. 1, AU sec. 324), was changed from *Reports on the Processing of Transactions by Service Organizations* by the issuance of SAS No. 78, *Consideration of Internal Control in a Financial Statement Audit: An Amendment to SAS No. 55* (AICPA, *Professional Standards*, vol. 1, AU sec. 319), and SAS No. 88, *Service Organizations and Reporting on Consistency*. SAS No. 70 was also amended by SAS No. 98, *Omnibus Statement on Auditing Standards—2002*, issued in September 2002. Throughout this Guide, SAS No. 70, as amended by SAS No. 78, No. 88, and No. 98, is referred to as SAS No. 70, as amended.

Of Internal Control Over Financial Reporting Performed In Conjunction With An Audit of Financial Statements."[†] The PCAOB has also issued three new auditing standards. These standards include:

- PCAOB Auditing Standard No. 1, *References in Auditors' Reports to the Standards of the Public Company Accounting Oversight Board*
- PCAOB Auditing Standard No. 2, *An Audit of Internal Control Over Financial Reporting Performed in Conjunction With an Audit of Financial Statements*
- PCAOB Auditing Standard No. 3, *Audit Documentation*

**I-05** Since this Guide is designed to provide guidance to service auditors engaged to issue reports on a service organization's controls that may be part of a user organization's information system in the context of an audit of financial statements and to provide guidance to user auditors engaged to audit the financial statements of entities that use service organizations, PCAOB Auditing Standards No. 1, 2 and 3 are not reflected in this guide, except to reflect certain conforming amendments made by PCAOB Release 2004-008 to certain of the interim standards discussed in this guide. For issuers, these conforming amendments have been footnoted throughout this guide, as applicable. Certain of the provisions in Release 2004-008 are relevant to situations in which an auditor is engaged solely to audit a company's financial statements and not just when performing an integrated audit of financial statements and internal control over financial reporting ("integrated audit"). For information on PCAOB auditing standards, quality control standards, and related guidance that may have been issued subsequent to the writing of this Guide, please refer to the PCAOB Web site at www.pcaobus.org (audits of issuers only).

## Applicability of SAS No. 70, as Amended

**I-06** SAS No. 70, as amended, is not applicable to every service provided by a service organization. It is applicable only if the service is part of the user organization's *information system*. A service organization's services are part of an entity's information system if they affect any of the following:

- The classes of transactions in the entity's operations that are significant to the financial statements.
- The procedures, both automated and manual, by which the entity's transactions are initiated, recorded, processed, and reported from their occurrence to their inclusion in the financial statements.
- The related accounting records, whether electronic or manual, supporting information, and specific accounts in the financial statements involved in initiating, recording, processing and reporting the entity's transactions.
- How the entity's information system captures other events and conditions that are significant to the financial statements.
- The financial reporting process used to prepare the entity's financial statements, including significant accounting estimates and disclosures.

---

[†] See the PCAOB web site at www.pcaobus.org for information about the effective date of these conforming amendments.

**I-07** The guidance in SAS No. 70, as amended, is not relevant to situations in which:

- The services provided are limited to executing client organization transactions that are specifically authorized by the client, such as the processing of checking account transactions by a bank or the execution of securities transactions by a broker.
- The audit of transactions arising from financial interests in partnerships, corporations, and joint ventures, such as working interests in oil and gas ventures, when proprietary interests are accounted for and reported to interest holders.

## Definitions

**I-08** Readers of this Guide should be familiar with the following terms, which are defined in SAS No. 70, as amended.

- *User organization.* The entity that has engaged a service organization and whose financial statements are being audited.
- *User auditor.* The auditor who reports on the financial statements of the user organization.
- *Service organization.* The entity (or segment of an entity) that provides services to a user organization that are part of the user organization's information system.
- *Service auditor.* The auditor who reports on controls of a service organization that may be relevant to a user organization's internal control as it relates to an audit of financial statements.

**I-09** The concept of an entity's internal control is fundamental to SAS No. 70, as amended, and is defined in SAS No. 55, *Consideration of Internal Control in a Financial Statement Audit*, as amended (AICPA, *Professional Standards*, vol. 1, AU sec. 319).[2] An entity's internal control consists of five interrelated components: control environment, risk assessment, control activities, information and communication, and monitoring. Internal control is also defined as a process designed to provide reasonable assurance regarding the achievement of objectives in the following categories:

- Reliability of financial reporting
- Effectiveness and efficiency of operations
- Compliance with applicable laws and regulations

**I-10** There is a direct relationship between these objectives, which are what the entity strives to achieve, and the components, which represent what

---

[2] In December 1995, SAS No. 55, *Consideration of Internal Control in a Financial Statement Audit* (AICPA, *Professional Standards*, vol. 1, AU sec. 319), was amended by the issuance of SAS No. 78. SAS No. 78 revises the definition and description of internal control contained in SAS No. 55 to recognize the definition and description contained in *Internal Control—Integrated Framework*, published by the Committee of Sponsoring Organizations of the Treadway Commission. In May 2001, SAS No. 55 was amended to reflect the issuance of SAS No. 94, *The Effect of Information Technology on the Auditor's Consideration of Internal Control in a Financial Statement Audit* (AICPA, *Professional Standards*, vol. 1, AU sec. 319). SAS No. 94 amends SAS No. 55 to provide guidance to auditors about the effect of information technology on internal control, and on the auditor's understanding of internal control and assessment of control risk. This Guide reflects the paragraph renumbering introduced by SAS No. 94. Throughout this Guide, SAS No. 55 as amended by SAS No. 78 and No. 94 is referred to as SAS No. 55, as amended.

is needed to achieve the objectives. Controls that are relevant to an audit of financial statements generally pertain to the entity's objective of reliable financial reporting, that is, preparing financial statements for external purposes that are fairly presented in conformity with generally accepted accounting principles or a comprehensive basis of accounting other than generally accepted accounting principles.[3] SAS No. 70, as amended, addresses the effect that a service organization may have on an entity's financial reporting objectives. Controls related to the operations and compliance objectives may be relevant to an audit of financial statements if they pertain to information the auditor evaluates or uses in applying auditing procedures.

I-11    This Guide focuses on a user organization's internal control, rather than a service organization's internal control, because a service organization's internal control is relevant to its own financial statement reporting objectives and not to the services it provides to user organizations. The following are definitions of certain terms used in this Guide.

- *Controls.* The policies and procedures an entity establishes to implement one or more aspects of the five components of internal control. Controls that affect a user organization's financial statements may exist at the user organization *or* at the service organization because when a user organization uses a service organization, certain controls at the service organization may be part of the user organization's information system.

- *Service organization's controls.* Controls at a service organization that may be part of a user organization's information system in the context of an audit of the user organization's financial statements. They do not include service organization controls that are not relevant to a user organization's information system.

- *Control objectives.* Generally, financial statement reporting control objectives, but also may encompass compliance or operational control objectives.

---

[3] SAS No. 62, *Special Reports* (AICPA, *Professional Standards*, vol. 1, AU sec. 623.04), defines a comprehensive basis of accounting other than generally accepted accounting principles.

# TABLE OF CONTENTS

**Contents**

**Contents**

Contents

Chapter 1

# Audit Considerations for an Entity That Uses a Service Organization*

**1.01** *This chapter identifies the information a user auditor may need about the processing performed by a service organization for a user organization and also describes how a user auditor obtains that information.*

## Applying SAS No. 55, as Amended, to the Audit of a User Organization's Financial Statements

**1.02** SAS No. 55, *Consideration of Internal Control in a Financial Statement Audit*, as amended (AICPA, *Professional Standards*, vol. 1, AU sec. 319),[1] states that internal control is a process effected by an entity's board of directors, management, and other personnel designed to provide reasonable assurance regarding the achievement of objectives in the following categories: (1) reliability of financial reporting, (2) effectiveness and efficiency of operations, and (3) compliance with applicable laws and regulations. Internal control consists of the following five interrelated components:

1. *Control environment* sets the tone of an organization, influencing the control consciousness of its people. It is the foundation for all the other components of internal control, providing discipline and structure.

2. *Risk assessment* is the entity's identification and analysis of relevant risks to the achievement of its objectives, forming a basis for determining how the risks should be managed.

3. *Control activities* are the policies and procedures that help ensure that management directives are carried out.

4. *Information and communication* systems support the identification, capture, and exchange of information in a form and time frame that enable people to carry out their responsibilities.

5. *Monitoring* is a process that assesses the quality of internal control performance over time.

---

* Refer to the Preface of this Guide for important information about the applicability of the professional standards to audits of issuers and non-issuers (see definitions in the Preface). As applicable, this chapter contains dual referencing to both the AICPA and the PCAOB's professional standards. See the PCAOB web site at www.pcaobus.org for information about the effective date of Auditing Standard No. 2 and related conforming amendments.

[1] In December 1995, Statement on Auditing Standards (SAS) No. 55, *Consideration of Internal Control in a Financial Statement Audit* (AICPA, *Professional Standards*, vol. 1, AU sec. 319), was amended by the issuance of SAS No. 78, *Consideration of Internal Control in a Financial Statement Audit: An Amendment to SAS No. 55* (AICPA, *Professional Standards*, vol. 1, AU sec. 319). SAS No. 78 revises the definition and description of internal control contained in SAS No. 55 to recognize the definition and description contained in *Internal Control—Integrated Framework*, published by the Committee of Sponsoring Organizations of the Treadway Commission. In May 2001, SAS No. 55 was amended to reflect the issuance of SAS No. 94, *The Effect of Information Technology on the Auditor's Consideration of Internal Control in a Financial Statement Audit*. SAS No. 94 amends SAS No. 55 to provide guidance to auditors about the effect of information technology on internal control, and on the auditor's understanding of internal control and assessment of control risk. This Guide reflects the paragraph renumbering introduced by SAS No. 94. Throughout this Guide, SAS No. 55 as amended by SAS No. 78 and No. 94 is referred to as SAS No. 55, as amended.

**1.03** In all audits, the auditor should obtain an understanding of internal control sufficient to plan the audit by performing procedures to understand the design of controls relevant to an audit of financial statements, and determining whether they have been placed in operation. In obtaining this understanding, the auditor considers how an entity's use of information technology (IT) and manual procedures may affect controls relevant to the audit. The auditor then assesses control risk for the assertions[2] embodied in the account balance, transaction class, and disclosure components of the financial statements.[3]

**1.04** If an organization uses a service organization, transactions that affect the user organization's financial statements are subjected to controls that may be physically and operationally removed from the user organization. Consequently, a user organization's internal control may include controls that are not directly administered by the user organization. For this reason, planning the audit may require that a user auditor gain an understanding of controls at the service organization that may affect the user organization's financial statements. This understanding may be gained in several ways, including obtaining a service auditor's report. The fact that an entity uses a service organization is not, in and of itself, a compelling reason for a user auditor to conclude that it is necessary to obtain a service auditor's report to plan the audit. Factors to consider in determining whether a user auditor should obtain a service auditor's report are presented in the following section.

## The Effect of a Service Organization on a User Organization's Internal Control and Planning the Audit of a User Organization's Financial Statements[4]

**1.05** The guidance in SAS No. 70, *Service Organizations*, as amended (AICPA, *Professional Standards*, vol. 1, AU sec. 324), is applicable to the audit of the financial statements of an entity that obtains services from another organization that are part of the user organization's information system. A service organization's services are part of an entity's information system if they affect any of the following:

- The classes of transactions in the entity's operations that are significant to the financial statements.

- The procedures, both automated and manual, by which transactions are initiated, recorded, processed, and reported from their occurrence to their inclusion in the financial statements.

---

[2] For issuers, the term "assertions" is replaced with "relevant assertions." See PCAOB Release 2004-008 and AICPA publication, *PCAOB Standards and Related Rules*, AU sec. 319.

[3] For issuers, regardless of the assessed level of control risk, the auditor should perform substantive procedures for all relevant assertions related to all significant accounts and disclosures in the financial statements. Refer to paragraphs 68-70 of PCAOB Auditing Standard No. 2 for discussion of identifying relevant financial statement assertions. (See PCAOB Release 2004-008 and AICPA publication, *PCAOB Standards and Related Rules*, AU sec. 319.)

[4] SAS No. 70, *Service Organizations*, as amended (AICPA, *Professional Standards*, vol. 1, AU sec. 324.06–.10), provides guidance on the effect of a service organization on a user organization's internal control, and planning the audit of a user organization's financial statements. For issuers, when performing an integrated audit, refer to paragraphs B18-B29 of Appendix B, "Additional Performance Requirements and Directions; Extent-Of-Testing Examples," in PCAOB Auditing Standard No. 2 regarding the use of service organizations. (See PCAOB Release 2004-008 and AICPA publication, *PCAOB Standards and Related Rules*, AU sec. 324).

- The related accounting records, whether electronic or manual, supporting information, and specific accounts in the financial statements involved in initiating, recording, processing and reporting transactions.
- How the information system captures other events and conditions that are significant to the financial statements.
- The financial reporting process used to prepare the entity's financial statements, including significant accounting estimates and disclosures.

## Examples of Service Organizations

**1.06**   As previously stated, SAS No. 55, as amended, requires an auditor to obtain a sufficient understanding of an entity's internal control to plan the audit. In certain situations, an entity's internal control extends beyond the controls within its physical facility or internal operations. This can happen if an entity uses another organization to perform services that are a part of the entity's information system. SAS No. 70, as amended, refers to these organizations as service organizations. The following are some examples of service organizations:

- *Trust departments of banks and insurance companies.* The trust department of a bank or an insurance company may provide a wide range of services to user organizations such as employee benefit plans. This type of service organization could be given authority to make decisions about how a plan's assets are invested. It also may serve as custodian of the plan's assets, maintain records of each participant's account, allocate investment income to the participants based on a formula in the trust agreement, make distributions to the participants, and prepare filings for the plan, such as Form 5500, "Internal Revenue Service Annual Return/Report of Employee Benefit Plan." If an employee benefit plan engages a service organization to perform some or all of these tasks, the services provided by the service organization may be part of the plan's information system and may have a significant effect on the plan's financial statements.

- *Transfer agents, custodians, and recordkeepers for investment companies.* Transfer agents process purchases, sales, and other shareholder activity for investment companies. Shareholders or prospective shareholders of investment companies initiate transactions by contacting the transfer agent either in writing, by telephone through an automated response unit, or through the Internet. The transfer agent remits to (receives from) the investment company the net proceeds from the purchase and sale of shares in the investment company. The custodian is responsible for the receipt, delivery, and safekeeping of the company's portfolio securities; the receipt and disbursement of cash resulting from transactions in these securities; and the maintenance of records of the securities held for the investment company. The custodian also may perform other services for the investment company, such as collecting dividend and interest income and distributing that income to the investment company. Recordkeepers maintain the financial accounting records of the investment company based on information provided by the transfer agent and the custodian of the investment company's investments. From the perspective of the investment company, the transfer agent, custodian performing servicing, and recordkeeper may be service organizations. Accordingly, auditors of an investment company may obtain information from a service auditor's report on controls at a transfer agent, recordkeeper, and custodian. From the perspective of an investor, an investment company is not a service organization but rather an entity in which the investor has a financial interest; accordingly, SAS No. 70, as amended, does not apply.

- *Insurers that maintain the accounting for ceded reinsurance.* Reinsurance is the assumption by one insurer (the assuming company) of all or part of the risk originally undertaken by another insurer (the ceding company). Generally, the ceding company retains responsibility for claims processing and is reimbursed by the assuming company for claims paid. As noted in the AICPA Audit and Accounting Guide *Property and Liability Insurance Companies*, the assuming company should establish controls over the accuracy and reliability of data received from the ceding company. The auditor of the assuming company's financial statements should obtain an understanding of the assuming company's procedures for assessing the accuracy and reliability of the data received from the ceding company. As part of that process, the auditor of the assuming company's financial statements may wish to obtain a service auditor's report on the ceding company's controls over the processing of ceded reinsurance claims.

- *Mortgage servicers or depository institutions that service loans for others.* Investor organizations may purchase mortgage loans or participation interests in such loans from thrifts, banks, or mortgage companies. These loans become assets of the investor organizations, and the sellers continue to service the loans. Mortgage servicing activities generally include collecting mortgage payments from borrowers, conducting collection and foreclosure activities, maintaining escrow accounts for the payment of property taxes and insurance, paying taxing authorities and insurance companies as payments become due, remitting monies to investors (user organizations), and reporting data concerning the mortgage to user organizations. The user organizations may have little or no contact with the mortgage servicer other than receiving the monthly payments and reports from the mortgage servicer. The user organizations record transactions related to the underlying mortgage loans based on data provided by the mortgage servicer. Auditors of the financial statements of mortgage investors may obtain information from a service auditor's report on controls related to the servicing of mortgages.

- *Application service providers (ASPs).* Application service providers generally provide packaged software applications and a technology environment that enables customers to process financial and operational transactions. An ASP may specialize in providing a particular software package solution to its users, may provide services similar to traditional mainframe data center service bureaus, may perform business processes for user organizations that they traditionally had performed themselves, or some combination of these services. As such, an ASP may provide services that are part of the entity's information system.

- *Internet service providers (ISPs) and Web hosting service providers.* Internet service providers enable user organizations to connect to the

Internet. Web hosting service providers generally develop, maintain, and operate Web sites for user organizations. The services provided by such entities may be part of a user organization's information system if the user organization is using the Internet or Web site to process transactions. If so, the user organization's information system may be affected by certain controls maintained by the ISP or Web hosting service provider, such as controls over the completeness and accuracy of the recording of transactions and controls over access to the system. For example, if a user organization takes orders and accepts payments through the Web site, certain controls maintained by the Web hosting service provider, such as controls over security access and controls that address the completeness and accuracy of the recording of transactions, may affect the user's information system.

- *Regional transmission organizations (RTOs)*. The electric utility industry is restructuring with a new class of entities referred to as RTOs, which include entities referred to as independent system operators that are responsible for the operation of a centrally dispatched electric system or wholesale electric market. They also are responsible for initiating, recording, billing, settling, and reporting transactions as well as collecting and remitting cash from participants based on the transmission tariff or other governing rules. These services may be part of a participant's information system. Auditors of the financial statements of participants may obtain a service auditor's report on controls related to participant settlement activity.

**1.07**    The list of service organizations presented in paragraph 1.06 is not intended to be a comprehensive list; many other types of entities also may function as service organizations. SAS No. 70, as amended (AU sec. 324.03), indicates that SAS No. 70, as amended, also may be relevant to situations in which an organization develops, provides, and maintains the software used by client organizations.

**1.08**    In the Internet economy, start-up organizations may outsource many or most functions affecting their information systems to minimize their initial capital outlay and the time required to commence operations. Controls at organizations that provide services such as order processing, warehousing, financial systems processing, and financial recordkeeping to start-up organizations may affect the start-up organization's information system. In view of the constantly expanding use of service organizations, auditors of entities should consider whether and the extent to which the entity uses other service organizations for functions that affect its information system and internal control.

**1.09**    SAS No. 55, *Consideration of Internal Control in a Financial Statement Audit,* as amended, states that an auditor should obtain an understanding of an entity's internal control sufficient to plan the audit. This understanding may encompass controls placed in operation by the entity and by service organizations whose services are part of the entity's information system. In planning the audit, such knowledge should be used to:

- Identify types of potential misstatements.
- Consider factors that affect the risk of material misstatement.

- Design tests of controls, when applicable. SAS No. 55, as amended (AU sec. 319.65–.69), discusses factors the auditor considers in determining whether to perform tests of controls.[5]
- Design substantive tests.

**1.10** When a user organization uses a service organization, transactions that affect the user organization's financial statements are subjected to controls that are, at least in part, physically and operationally separate from the user organization.

**1.11** When planning the audit of a user organization's financial statements, a user auditor should determine the significance of the service organization's controls to the user organization's internal control and the assertions embodied in the user organization's financial statements. If the user auditor determines that the service organization's controls are significant to the user organization's internal control and financial statement assertions, the user auditor should gain a sufficient understanding of those controls to plan the audit, as required by SAS No. 55, as amended. Several factors may affect the significance of a service organization's controls to a user organization's internal control and financial statement assertions. The most important factors are the following.

- *The nature and materiality of the transactions or accounts affected by the service organization.* If the transactions processed or accounts affected by the service organization are material to the user organization's financial statements, the user auditor may need to obtain an understanding of the controls at the service organization. In certain situations, the transactions processed and the accounts affected by the service organization may not appear to be material to the user organization's financial statements, but the nature of the transactions processed may require that the user auditor obtain an understanding of those controls. Such a situation might exist when a service organization provides third-party administration services to self-insured organizations providing health insurance benefits to employees. Although transactions processed and accounts affected may not appear to be material to the user organization's financial statements, the user auditor may need to gain an understanding of the controls at the third-party administrator because improper processing may result in a material understatement of the liability for unpaid claims.
- *The degree of interaction between internal control at the user organization and the service organization's controls.* The degree of interaction refers to the extent to which a user organization is able to and elects to implement effective controls over the processing performed by the service organization. The degree of interaction depends on the nature of the services provided by the service organization. If the services provided by the service organization are limited to recording user organization transactions and processing the related data, and the user organization retains responsibility for authorizing the transactions and maintaining the related accountability, there will be a high degree of

---

[5] For issuers, when performing an integrated audit, if the auditor assesses control risk as other than low for certain assertions or significant accounts, the auditor should document the reasons for that conclusion. (See PCAOB Release 2004-008 and AICPA publication, *PCAOB Standards and Related Rules*, AU sec. 319.65).

interaction. In these circumstances, it may be practicable for the user organization to implement effective controls over those transactions. This can be exemplified by a situation in which an employee benefit plan uses the trust department of a bank to invest and maintain custody of its assets in a *directed* trust. In a directed trust, the employee benefit plan instructs the bank trust department to execute specific transactions, such as the purchase and sale of securities. The trust department is not permitted to initiate and execute transactions without specific authorization from the employee benefit plan. Under such an arrangement, the employee benefit plan is able to independently generate records of its investment activities to be used for the preparation of financial statements, and also is able to independently reconcile its records to information received from the bank trust department, such as statements and advices. If the employee benefit plan retains responsibility for authorizing the transactions and for maintaining the related accountability by independently generating and maintaining records and reconciling them to information provided by the bank trust department, there will be a high degree of interaction. However, if the employee benefit plan authorizes the transactions and does not generate and maintain independent records of its investment activities and, instead, records its investment activities solely from information generated by the bank trust department, there will be a lower degree of interaction between the internal control of the user organization and the controls of the service organization.

Alternatively, in another situation, an employee benefit plan may establish a *discretionary* trust rather than a directed trust. In a discretionary trust, the bank trust department is given discretionary authority to invest the plan's assets. The trust department is authorized to initiate and execute transactions without prior authorization of each transaction by the employee benefit plan. Under this arrangement, the employee benefit plan must record investment activity from information provided by the trust department because the employee benefit plan has no means of independently generating a record of its transactions. In such a situation there will be a lower degree of interaction between the internal control of the user organization and the controls of the service organization.

**1.12** If an auditor is auditing financial statements that contain material assertions derived from a service organization's recordkeeping, and the user organization is unable to, or elects not to, implement effective internal control over the processing performed by the service organization (for example, there is a low degree of interaction), the auditor generally will need to obtain an understanding of the controls at the service organization that affect those transactions.

**1.13** SAS No. 70, *Service Organizations*, as amended (AU sec. 324.09),[6] states that information about the nature of the services provided by a service organization that are part of the user organization's information system and the service organization's controls over those services may be available from a wide

---

[6] Throughout this Guide, SAS No. 70, *Service Organizations* (AICPA, *Professional Standards*, vol. 1, AU sec. 324), as amended by SAS No. 78, No. 88, and No. 98, is referred to as SAS No. 70, as amended.

variety of sources, such as user manuals, system overviews, technical manuals, the contract between the user organization and the service organization, and reports by service auditors, internal auditors, or regulatory authorities on the service organization's controls. If the services and the service organization's controls over those services are highly standardized, information obtained through the user auditor's prior experience with the service organization may be helpful in planning the audit.

## Sources of Information About a Service Organization

**1.14** If a user auditor determines that the controls at a service organization are significant to planning the audit of the user organization, the user auditor should gain an understanding of the service organization's controls sufficient to plan the audit. That understanding may encompass controls placed in operation by the entity and by service organizations whose services are part of the entity's information system. In planning the audit, such knowledge should be used to:

- Identify the types of potential misstatements that could occur in the user organization's financial statement assertions affected by the service provided.
- Consider factors that affect the risk of material misstatement.
- Design tests of controls, when applicable. SAS No. 55, as amended (AU sec. 319.65–.69), discusses factors the auditor considers in determining whether to perform tests of controls.[7]
- Design substantive tests.

**1.15** In considering the various sources of information about a service organization, a user auditor should determine whether a service auditor's report is available from the service organization. Chapter 3 of this Guide, "Using Type 1 and Type 2 Reports," provides guidance on using such reports. After considering the available information, the user auditor may conclude that he or she has the means to obtain a sufficient understanding of internal control to plan the audit. If the user auditor concludes that information is not available to obtain a sufficient understanding to plan the audit, he or she may consider the following alternatives:

- Contacting the service organization, through the user organization, to obtain specific information
- Requesting that a service auditor be engaged to perform procedures that will supply the necessary information
- Visiting the service organization and performing such procedures

If the user auditor is unable to obtain sufficient evidence to achieve his or her audit objectives, the user auditor should qualify his or her opinion or disclaim an opinion on the financial statements because of a scope limitation.

---

[7] For issuers, when performing an integrated audit, if the auditor assesses control risk as other than low for certain assertions or significant accounts, the auditor should document the reasons for that conclusion. (See PCAOB Release 2004-008 and AICPA publication, *PCAOB Standards and Related Rules*, AU sec. 319.65).

# The User Auditor's Assessment of Control Risk[8]

**1.16**  After obtaining an understanding of internal control, a user auditor should assess control risk for the assertions[9] in the user organization's financial statements, including the assertions affected by the service organization.[10] In doing so, the user auditor may identify certain controls that, if operating effectively, would permit a user auditor to assess control risk below the maximum for assertions affected by the service organization. In certain situations, these controls may be implemented at the user organization. For example, an organization using a payroll service organization could compare the data submitted to the service organization with reports or information received from the service organization after the data has been processed. The user organization also could recompute a sample of the payroll amounts for clerical accuracy and could review the total amount of the payroll for reasonableness. If a user auditor determines that appropriate controls implemented at the user organization are operating effectively to prevent or detect material misstatements in the user organization's financial statements, the user auditor may be able to assess control risk below the maximum for the assertions affected by the service organization, without identifying and testing controls at the service organization.[11]

**1.17**  In other situations, controls may be implemented at the service organization. If they are operating effectively, either by themselves or in concert with controls at the user organization, they may support an assessed level of control risk below the maximum for financial statement assertions affected by those controls. For example, a trust department may implement a control requiring that internal records concerning securities held by an outside custodian periodically are reconciled to information provided by the custodian and that the security balances in customers' accounts periodically are reconciled to the trust department's custodial records.

**1.18**  A user auditor may identify relevant service organization controls by reading a description of the service organization's controls in a service auditor's report. Information about the effectiveness of such controls may be obtained from such a report if the report includes tests of operating effectiveness. If the service auditor's report does not include tests of operating effectiveness, the user auditor may contact the service organization, through the user organization, to request that a service auditor be engaged to perform a service auditor's examination that includes tests of the operating effectiveness of the relevant controls or to perform agreed-upon procedures[12] that test the operating

---

[8]  SAS No. 70, as amended (AU sec. 324.11–.16), provides guidance on assessing control risk at a user organization.

[9]  For issuers, the term "assertions" is replaced with "relevant assertions." See PCAOB Release 2004-008 and AICPA publication, *PCAOB Standards and Related Rules*, AU sec. 319.

[10]  For issuers, regardless of the assessed level of control risk, the auditor should perform substantive procedures for all relevant assertions related to all significant accounts and disclosures in the financial statements. Refer to paragraphs 68-70 of PCAOB Auditing Standard No. 2 for discussion of identifying relevant financial statement assertions. (See PCAOB Release 2004-008 and AICPA publication, *PCAOB Standards and Related Rules*, AU sec. 319.)

[11]  For issuers, when performing an integrated audit, if the auditor assesses control risk as other than low for certain assertions or significant accounts, the auditor should document the reasons for that conclusion. (See PCAOB Release 2004-008 and AICPA publication, *PCAOB Standards and Related Rules*, AU sec. 319.65).

[12]  Statement on Standards for Attestation Engagements (SSAE) No. 10, *Attestation Standards: Revision and Recodification* (AICPA, *Professional Standards*, vol. 1, AT sec. 201, "Agreed-Upon Procedures Engagements"), as amended, provides guidance for performing and reporting on such engagements.

effectiveness of those controls. A user auditor also may visit the service organization and perform procedures at the service organization if the service organization's management agrees to such an arrangement. In all cases, the user auditor's assessments regarding financial statement assertions are based on the combined evidence provided by the service auditor's report and the user auditor's procedures.

## Other Types of Internal Control Engagements

**1.19** In addition to SAS No. 70, as amended, the following professional standards provide guidance to practitioners who (1) report on aspects of an entity's internal control or (2) are required to identify and report certain conditions related to an entity's internal control observed during an audit of the entity's financial statements. The objectives and work products of these engagements differ from the objectives and work product of a service auditor's engagement because they do not provide a user auditor with the information as well as the assurance provided by a service auditor's report.

- *Statement on Standards for Attestation Engagements (SSAE) No. 10, Attestation Standards: Revision and Recodification (AICPA,* Professional Standards, *vol. 1, AT sec. 501, "Reporting on an Entity's Internal Control Over Financial Reporting").*[13] This section provides guidance to practitioners engaged to examine and report on (1) the effectiveness of an entity's internal control over financial reporting or (2) an assertion thereon. An entity's internal control over financial reporting includes those controls that pertain to an entity's ability to initiate, record, summarize, and report financial data consistent with the assertions embodied in its financial statements. In this type of engagement, the practitioner obtains an understanding of the entity's internal control over financial reporting, tests and evaluates the design and operating effectiveness of the controls, and expresses an opinion on (1) the effectiveness of the entity's internal control over financial reporting as of a specified date based on control criteria or (2) whether the responsible party's assertion about the effectiveness of internal control over financial reporting as of a specified date is fairly stated, based on the control criteria. Unlike a service auditor's report, which is designed to be used by a user auditor to plan an audit, it does not include a description of a service organization's controls or a description of tests of operating effectiveness and results of the tests. A report issued under SSAE No. 10 (AT sec. 501) is not intended to be used by a user auditor to plan the audit of a user organization's financial statements.

- *SSAE No. 10 (AICPA,* Professional Standards, *vol. 1, AT sec. 601, "Compliance Attestation").* This section provides guidance for engagements related to (1) an entity's compliance with requirements of specified laws, regulations, rules, contracts or grants; or (2) the effectiveness of an entity's internal control over compliance with specified requirements. Unlike a service auditor's report, which is designed to be used by a user auditor to plan an audit, it does not include a description

---

[13] For issuers, Chapter 5, "Reporting on an Entity's Internal Control Over Financial Reporting," of SSAE No. 10, *Attestation Standards: Revision and Codification* (AT sec. 501), and its related interpretation (AT sec. 9501) are superseded by the conforming amendments in PCAOB Release 2004-008 and, accordingly, are no longer interim standards of the PCAOB.

of the controls at a service organization or a description of tests of operating effectiveness and results of these tests.

- *SAS No. 60,* Communication of Internal Control Related Matters Noted in an Audit *(AICPA, Professional Standards, vol. 1, AU sec. 325).*[14] As part of an audit of an entity's financial statements, an auditor may be required to issue an internal control communication in accordance with the requirements of SAS No. 60. SAS No. 60 does not apply to a service auditor's engagement because it provides guidance on identifying and communicating reportable conditions that come to an auditor's attention during the audit of an entity's financial statements, to an audit committee or to individuals with a level of authority and responsibility equivalent to an audit committee.

**1.20** Certain engagements performed under SSAE No 10 address controls other than those related to financial reporting. Two examples of such engagements are:

- *SysTrust*[sm]. This is an assurance service in which a practitioner tests and reports on the effectiveness of controls over system reliability. The engagement addresses controls over system availability, security, integrity, and maintainability. The CPA reports on the effectiveness of the controls as measured against specified criteria for system availability, security, integrity, and maintainability. The intended users of these reports are management, customers, creditors, bankers, users who outsource functions to other entities, and anyone who in some way relies on the continued availability, security, integrity, and maintainability of a system. A SysTrust engagement differs from a service auditor's engagement in a number of ways. The following table highlights the differences between the two engagements.

| | SAS No. 70, as amended | SysTrust |
|---|---|---|
| Nature of the engagement | Provides a report on a service organization's controls related to financial statement assertions of user organizations | Provides a report on system reliability using standard principles and criteria for all engagements |
| Are there preestablished control objectives or criteria? | No | Yes |
| Objective of the engagement | Information sharing and assurance | Assurance on a system |
| | Provides detailed information on the design of the system and controls, and an opinion on the system description and controls | No detail on the underlying control procedures is provided |

---

[14] For issuers, SAS No. 60 has been superseded and its title changed to AU sec. 325, *Communications About Control Deficiencies in An Audit of Financial Statements.* For audits of financial statements only, SAS No. 60 has been superseded by certain paragraphs of PCAOB Release 2004-008. For integrated audits, SAS No. 60 has been superseded by paragraphs 207-214 of PCAOB Auditing Standard No. 2. (See AICPA, *PCAOB Standards and Related Rules,* AU sec. 325.)

| | SAS No. 70, as amended | SysTrust |
|---|---|---|
| Types of systems addressed by the engagement | Financial systems | Financial and nonfinancial systems |
| Audience for the report | Service organizations, user organizations, and auditors of the user organizations | Stakeholders of the system—for example, management, customers, and business partners |

- *WebTrust*<sup>sm</sup>. This is an attestation service in which a practitioner reports on management's assertion about a Web site. The WebTrust program is modular by design so a practitioner may report on various aspects of a Web site based on criteria established for online privacy, confidentiality, availability, business practices/transaction integrity, security, nonrepudiation, and certification authorities.

Chapter 2

# Form and Content of Service Auditors' Reports[*]

**2.01**  *This chapter describes the two types of service auditor's engagements that a service auditor may perform and describes the reports that are issued for each engagement. It also identifies the sections of each report and describes the information that should be included in each section.*

## Types of Service Auditors' Reports

**2.02**  A service auditor may provide a service organization with two types of reports:

1. A report on controls placed in operation, which will be referred to as *a type 1 report* in this Guide

2. A report on controls placed in operation and tests of operating effectiveness, which will be referred to as *a type 2 report* in this Guide.

**2.03**  The type of engagement to be performed should be determined by the service organization. However, if circumstances permit, discussions between the management of the service organization and the managements of the user organizations are advisable to determine the services or applications that will be covered by the report and the type of engagement and related report that will be most useful to the user organizations and their auditors.

## Format and Content of Type 1 and Type 2 Reports

**2.04**  Although the format of a type 1 or type 2 report is flexible, these reports always will contain the following information, ordinarily in the sections noted:

- Independent service auditor's report (section 1)
- Service organization's description of controls (section 2)

**2.05**  The following information will always appear in a type 2 report and may appear in a type 1 report, ordinarily in section 3:

- Information provided by the independent service auditor (section 3): This information always is included in a type 2 report because the service auditor must describe the tests of operating effectiveness that he or she has performed and the results of those tests. This section is optional in a type 1 report. Examples of information that might be included in this section are a more detailed description of the objectives of a service auditor's engagement or information relating to regulatory requirements.

---

[*] Refer to the Preface of this Guide for important information about the applicability of the professional standards to audits of issuers and non-issuers (see definitions in the Preface). As applicable, this chapter contains dual referencing to both the AICPA and the PCAOB professional standards. See the PCAOB web site at www.pcaobus.org for information about the effective date of PCAOB Auditing Standard No. 2 and related conforming amendments.

**2.06**   The following information is optional in a type 1 or type 2 report:

- Other information provided by the service organization (section 4). This information is optional in type 1 and type 2 reports. An example of such information is a service organization's plans for enhancing its systems.

**2.07**   Throughout the remainder of this Guide, the terms *type 1 report* and *type 2 report* will be used to refer to the entire document, that is, sections 1 and 2 and, if they are present, sections 3 and 4. The term *service auditor's report* will be used to refer only to section 1, which is the letter issued by the service auditor expressing an opinion on (1) the fairness of the presentation of the service organization's description of controls, (2) the suitability of the design of the controls to achieve specified control objectives, and (3) in a type 2 engagement—whether the specific controls were operating with sufficient effectiveness to achieve the related control objectives.

**2.08**   Although the format of a type 1 or type 2 report is flexible, the organization and presentation of the reports always should differentiate between (1) the service auditor's report (the letter issued by the service auditor), (2) the service organization's description of controls, (3) information provided by the service auditor, and (4) other information provided by the service organization to clearly indicate that:

- The service auditor is responsible for the representations in the service auditor's report (the letter issued by the service auditor in section 1) and for information provided by the service auditor (section 3).
- The service organization is responsible for the representations in the description of controls (section 2) and for other information provided by the service organization (section 4).

**2.09**   A service auditor's report (the letter issued by the service auditor) should not be distributed without the accompanying description of the service organization's controls, and when applicable, the description of the service auditor's tests of operating effectiveness and the results of those tests.

## The Independent Service Auditor's Report

**2.10**   In a type 1 engagement, the service auditor issues a report on a description of controls that has been prepared by the service organization. The service auditor makes inquiries of appropriate management, supervisory, and staff personnel; inspects documents and records; and observes activities at the service organization to gather evidence needed to express an opinion on whether the:

- Description presents fairly, in all material respects, the relevant aspects of the service organization's controls that had been placed in operation as of a specified date.
- Controls were suitably designed to provide reasonable assurance that the specified control objectives would be achieved if those controls were complied with satisfactorily.

**2.11**   A type 1 report is intended to provide user auditors with information about the controls at a service organization that may be relevant to a user organization's internal control as it relates to an audit of financial statements.

This information, in conjunction with other information about a user organization's internal control, should assist the user auditor in obtaining a sufficient understanding of the user organization's internal control to plan the audit, as described in Statement on Auditing Standards (SAS) No. 55, *Consideration of Internal Control in a Financial Statement Audit*, as amended (AICPA, *Professional Standards*, vol. 1, AU sec. 319.02 and .25–.61).[1] The user auditor obtains this understanding to enable him or her to (1) identify the types of misstatements that may occur in a user organization's financial statements; (2) consider the factors that affect the risk of material misstatement; (3) when applicable, design tests of controls; and (4) design substantive tests. *A type 1 report, however, is* not *intended to provide a user auditor with a basis for reducing his or her assessment of control risk below the maximum.* SAS No. 70, *Service Organizations*, as amended (AICPA, *Professional Standards*, vol. 1, AU sec. 324.38), presents an example of a service auditor's report for a type 1 engagement.

**2.12** In a type 2 engagement, the service auditor performs the procedures required for a type 1 engagement and also performs tests of specific controls to evaluate their operating effectiveness in achieving specified control objectives. Tests of operating effectiveness address how controls are applied, how consistently they are applied, and who applies them. The service auditor issues a report that includes the type 1 report opinions and refers the reader to a description of tests of operating effectiveness performed by a service auditor. The report states whether, in the opinion of the service auditor, the controls tested were operating with sufficient effectiveness to provide reasonable, but not absolute, assurance that the related control objectives were achieved during the period specified.

**2.13** If a service organization's controls (the controls that may affect a user organization's financial statements) are operating with sufficient effectiveness to achieve the related control objectives, a user auditor may be able to assess control risk below the maximum for certain financial statement assertions affected by the service organization's service or processing and, consequently, may be able to reduce the extent of substantive procedures performed for those assertions. To assess control risk below the maximum, a user auditor should consider the operating effectiveness of the relevant service organization controls in conjunction with the user organization's internal control. In considering the operating effectiveness of the relevant controls at the service organization, the user auditor should read and consider *both* the service auditor's:

1. Report on the operating effectiveness of the controls.
2. Description of the tests of the operating effectiveness of controls that may be relevant to specified assertions in the user organization's financial statements, and the results of those tests.

**2.14** *Under no circumstances should the service auditor's report (the letter issued by the service auditor) be the only basis for reducing the assessed level of control risk below the maximum.* The user auditor should read and consider both the report and the evidence provided by the tests of operating effectiveness and relate them to the assertions in the user organization's financial statements. Although a type 2 report may be used to reduce substantive procedures, neither a

---

[1] For issuers, certain paragraphs of SAS No. 55 have been amended by PCAOB Release 2004-008. See PCAOB Release 2004-008 or the AICPA, *PCAOB Standards and Related Rules*, AU sec. 319 for further guidance.

type 1 report nor a type 2 report is designed to provide a basis for assessing control risk sufficiently low to eliminate the need for performing any substantive tests for all of the assertions relevant to significant account balances or transaction classes. SAS No. 70, as amended (AU sec. 324.54), presents an example of a service auditor's report for a type 2 engagement.

**2.15**   Table 2-1 summarizes the service auditor's opinions included in each type of service auditor's report.

## Table 2-1

### Service Auditor's Opinions Included in Type 1 and Type 2 Service Auditors' Reports

| Opinion | Type 1 Report | Type 2 Report |
| --- | --- | --- |
| (1) Whether the service organization's description of its controls presents fairly, in all material respects, the relevant aspects of the service organization's controls that had been placed in operation as of a specific date | Included | Included |
| (2) Whether the controls were suitably designed to achieve specified control objectives | Included | Included |
| (3) Whether the controls that were tested were operating with sufficient effectiveness to provide reasonable, but not absolute, assurance that the control objectives were achieved during the period specified | Not included | Included |

## Use of a Service Auditor's Report

**2.16**   SAS No. 70, as amended (AU sec. 324.29h and .44m), requires that a service auditor's report contain a paragraph identifying the parties for whom the report is intended. Such a paragraph is presented in the illustrative service auditor's reports in paragraphs 5.28 and 5.30 of this Guide. The final paragraph of those reports state:

> This report is intended solely for use by the management of XYZ Service Organization, its customers, and the independent auditors of its customers.[2]

The authorized users of the report include only *present* users of the service organization and do not include *potential* users of the service organization.

## The Service Organization's Description of Controls

**2.17**   The service organization's description of controls generally is prepared by the service organization. The service organization is responsible for the completeness, accuracy, and method of presentation of the description. If the service auditor assists the service organization in preparing the description,

---

[2] Statement on Auditing Standards (SAS) No. 87, *Restricting the Use of an Auditor's Report* (AICPA, *Professional Standards*, vol. 1, AU sec. 532.19c) contains the following illustrative restricted-use paragraph: This report is intended solely for the information and use of [the specified parties] and is not intended to be and should not be used by anyone other than these specified parties.
    The language in that paragraph may be used in a service auditor's report.

the representations in the description remain the responsibility of the service organization. The description should provide user auditors with information about the service organization's controls that may be relevant to a user organization's internal control. Service organization controls are considered relevant to a user organizations' internal control if they represent or affect a user organization's internal control as it relates to an audit of financial statements. These service organization controls may represent or affect a user organization's control environment, risk assessment, control activities, information and communication, or monitoring components of internal control.

**2.18** The description of controls should be presented at a level of detail that provides user auditors with sufficient information to plan the audit as described in SAS No. 70, as amended (AU sec. 324.07), and SAS No. 55, as amended (AU sec. 319.26–.61).[3] The description need not address every aspect of the service organization's processing or the services provided to user organizations. Certain aspects of the processing or the services provided may not be relevant to user organizations and their auditors or may be beyond the scope of the engagement. For example, a service organization that provides five different applications to user organizations may engage a service auditor to report on only three of those applications. Similarly, a trust department that has separate organizational units providing personal trust services and institutional trust services may engage a service auditor to report only on the institutional trust services. In these situations, the service organization's description should address only the controls pertaining to those applications or organizational units included in the scope of the engagement.

**2.19** The service organization's description of controls generally should contain the following information:

- Aspects of the service organization's control environment; risk assessment; information and communication; and monitoring that may affect the services provided to user organizations, as it relates to an audit of financial statements
- Control objectives and related controls
- Changes to controls since the later of the date of the last report or within the last 12 months

## Aspects of the Control Environment That May Affect the Services Provided to User Organizations

**2.20** The control environment sets the tone of an organization, influencing the control consciousness of its people. It is the foundation for all the other components of internal control, providing discipline and structure. Aspects of a service organization's control environment may affect the services provided to user organizations. For example, management's hiring and training practices generally would be considered an aspect of the control environment that may affect the services provided to user organizations because those practices

---

[3] For issuers, certain paragraphs of SAS No. 55 have been amended by PCAOB Release 2004-008. See PCAOB Release 2004-008 or the AICPA Publication, *PCAOB Standards and Related Rules*, AU sec. 319 for further guidance.

# 18 Service Organizations: Applying SAS No. 70

affect the ability of service organization personnel to provide services to user organizations. SAS No. 55, as amended (AU sec. 319.34), provides the following examples of control environment factors:

- Integrity and ethical values
- Commitment to competence
- Board of directors or audit committee participation
- Management's philosophy and operating style
- Organizational structure
- Assignment of authority and responsibility
- Human resource policies and practices

**2.21** Only relevant control environment factors that affect the services provided to user organizations should be described in this section of the report. Ordinarily, control environment factors are not presented in the form of control objectives because of their nature; however, management is not precluded from presenting relevant aspects of its control environment in the context of control objectives.

## Aspects of the Risk Assessment Process That May Affect the Services Provided to User Organizations

**2.22** Aspects of a service organization's risk assessment process may affect the services provided to user organizations. As discussed in SAS No. 55, as amended, an entity's risk assessment process pertains to its own financial reporting. However, a service organization also may have a risk assessment process that addresses services provided to user organizations. How management of a service organization addresses identified risks could affect its own financial-reporting process as well as the financial-reporting process of the user organizations. SAS No. 55, as amended (AU sec. 319.38), identifies circumstances that may affect risk. Following are a list of those factors and examples of how they might relate to a service organization.

- *Changes in the operating environment.* If a service organization provides services to user organizations in a regulated industry, a change in regulations may necessitate a revision of existing processing. Revisions of existing processing may create the need for additional or revised controls.
- *New personnel.* New personnel who are responsible for executing manual controls that affect user organizations may increase the risk that controls will not operate effectively.
- *New or revamped information systems.* A service organization may incorporate new functions into its system that could affect user organizations.
- *Rapid growth.* If a service organization gains a substantial number of new customers, the operating effectiveness of certain controls could be affected.
- *New technology.* A service organization may implement a client-server version of its software that was previously run on a mainframe. Although the new software may perform similar functions, it may operate so differently that it affects user organizations.

**AAG-SRV 2.21**

- *New business models, products, or activities.* The diversion of resources to new activities from existing activities could affect certain controls at a service organization.
- *Corporate restructurings.* A change in ownership or internal reorganization could affect reporting responsibilities or the resources available for services to user organizations.
- *Expanded foreign operations.* A service organization that uses personnel in foreign locations to maintain programs used by domestic user organizations may have difficulty responding to changes in user requirements.
- *New accounting pronouncements.* The implementation of relevant accounting pronouncements in a service organization's software and controls could affect user organizations.

**2.23**    Only relevant aspects of the risk assessment process that affect the services provided to user organizations should be described in this section of the report. Ordinarily, relevant aspects of the risk assessment process are not presented in the form of control objectives because of their nature. However, management is not precluded from presenting relevant aspects of its risk assessment in the context of control objectives.

## Aspects of Information and Communication That May Affect a User Organization's Internal Control

**2.24**    Activities of a service organization that may represent a user organization's information and communication component of internal control include the procedures, whether automated or manual, and records established by the service organization to:

- Initiate, record, process, and report a user organization's transactions (as well as events and conditions) and maintain accountability for the related assets, liabilities, and equity.[4]
- Provide an understanding of the individual roles and responsibilities pertaining to internal control over financial reporting.

**2.25**    SAS No. 55, as amended (AU sec. 319.49), states that the auditor should obtain sufficient knowledge of the information system relevant to financial reporting to understand:

- The classes of transactions in the entity's operations that are significant to the financial statements.

---

[4] Paragraph 12 of the appendix to SAS No. 55, *Consideration of Internal Control in a Financial Statement Audit*, as amended (AICPA, *Professional Standards*, vol. 1, AU sec. 319.110), states: The information system relevant to financial reporting objectives, which includes the accounting system, consists of the procedures, whether automated or manual, and records established to initiate, record, process, and report entity transactions (as well as events and conditions) and to maintain accountability for the related assets, liabilities, and equity. Transactions may be initiated manually or automatically by programmed procedures. Recording includes identifying and capturing the relevant information for transactions or events. Processing includes functions such as edit and validation, calculation, measurement, valuation, summarization, and reconciliation, whether performed by automated or manual procedures. Reporting relates to the preparation of financial reports as well as other information, in electronic or printed format, that the entity uses in monitoring and other functions. The quality of system-generated information affects management's ability to make appropriate decisions in managing and controlling the entity's activities and to prepare reliable financial reports.

- The procedures, both automated and manual, by which transactions are initiated, recorded, processed, and reported from their occurrence to their inclusion in the financial statements.
- The related accounting records, whether electronic or manual; supporting information; and specific accounts in the financial statements involved in initiating, recording, processing and reporting transactions.
- How the information system captures other events and conditions that are significant to the financial statements.
- The financial reporting process used to prepare the entity's financial statements, including significant accounting estimates and disclosures.

**2.26**   The auditor also should obtain sufficient knowledge of the means the service organization uses to communicate individual roles and responsibilities pertaining to controls that may affect the services provided to user organizations. This may include the extent to which service organization personnel understand how their activities relate to the work of others (including user organizations) and the means for reporting exceptions to an appropriate higher level within the service organization and to user organizations.

## Aspects of Monitoring That May Affect the Services Provided to User Organizations

**2.27**   SAS No. 55, as amended (AU sec. 319.54), describes the monitoring process. Many aspects of monitoring may be relevant to the services provided to user organizations. For example, a service organization may employ internal auditors or other personnel to evaluate the quality of control performance over time, either by ongoing activities, periodic evaluations, or various combinations of the two. Monitoring external communications, such as customer complaints and communications from regulators, generally would be relevant to the services provided to user organizations.

**2.28**   Only relevant aspects of monitoring that affect the services provided to user organizations should be described in this section of the report. Ordinarily, relevant aspects of monitoring are not presented in the form of control objectives; however, management is not precluded from presenting those aspects in the context of control objectives.

## Level of Detail of the Description of Controls

**2.29**   The service organization's description of controls should provide sufficient information for user auditors to understand how the service organization's processing affects the components described in the preceding sections. The degree of detail of the description should be equivalent to the degree of detail a user auditor would require if a service organization were not used. However, it need not be so detailed as to potentially allow a reader to compromise security or other controls. For example, it should describe the classes of transactions that are processed, but not necessarily each individual transaction type. It need not necessarily include every step in the processing of the transactions and may be presented in various formats such as narratives, flowcharts, tables, and graphics. The description also should indicate the extent of the manual and computer processing used.

## Control Objectives, Related Controls, and Assertions in User Organizations' Financial Statements

**2.30**  This section describes a service organization's control objectives and how they relate to the service organization's controls and to the assertions in user organizations' financial statements.

**2.31**  A service organization's control objectives should be tailored to the service provided by the service organization. The control objectives help the user auditor determine how the service organization's controls affect the user organization's financial statement assertions. SAS No. 31, *Evidential Matter* (AICPA, *Professional Standards*, vol. 1, AU sec. 326), states that assertions are representations by management that are embodied in financial statement components. They can be either explicit or implicit and can be classified according to the following broad categories:

- Existence or occurrence
- Completeness
- Rights and obligations
- Valuation or allocation
- Presentation and disclosure

**2.32**  Although the management of a service organization will not be able to determine how a service organization's controls specifically relate to the assertions embodied in all the user organizations' financial statements, it should be able to identify the types of assertions to which its controls are likely to relate. The service organization should establish control objectives (1) that it believes relate to those assertions, and (2) that provide a framework for user auditors to assess the effect of the service organization's controls on those assertions. The following are examples of how a service organization's controls relate to assertions in a user organization's financial statements.

### Example 1

**2.33**  In the sample type 2 report for Example Computer Service Organization, presented in Appendix A of this Guide, the service organization provides computer services to user organizations in the financial services industry. Example Computer Service Organization has engaged a service auditor to report on its description of controls related to its savings, mortgage loan, and consumer loan applications. For the savings application, the service organization maintains the detailed records of savings account balances and processes related transactions affecting those balances. It also calculates interest and penalty amounts and produces reports that are provided to user organizations for use in the preparation of their financial statements.

**2.34**  The service organization has specified control objectives that it believes relate to assertions in the user organizations' financial statements and that are consistent with its contractual obligations. Table 2-2 indicates the control objectives specified by the service organization and the types of assertions in the user organizations' financial statements to which they relate.

## Table 2-2

### Examples of Assertions in User Organizations' Financial Statements and Related Service Organization Control Objectives *

| Assertions in User Organizations' Financial Statements | Control Objectives of the Service Organization |
|---|---|
| | Controls provide reasonable assurance that— |
| Existence or occurrence | Savings deposits and withdrawal transactions are received from authorized sources. |
| | Data maintained on files remain authorized, complete, and accurate. |
| Completeness | Savings deposit and withdrawal transactions received from the user organizations initially are recorded completely and accurately. |
| | Output data and documents are complete and accurate and distributed to authorized recipients on a timely basis. |
| Valuation or allocation | Programmed interest and penalties are calculated in conformity with the description. |
| | Output data and documents are complete and accurate and distributed to authorized recipients on a timely basis. |

* *Source:* Sample type 2 report for Example Computer Service Organization presented in Appendix A.

## Example 2

**2.35**   In the sample type 2 report for Example Trust Organization presented in Appendix A, the service organization provides fiduciary services to institutional, corporate, and personal trust customers. Example Trust Organization has engaged a service auditor to report on its description of controls related to its processing of transactions for user organizations of the institutional trust division. Example Trust Organization has discretionary authority over investment activities, maintains the detailed records of investment transactions, and records investment income and expense. Reports are provided to user organizations for use in the preparation of their financial statements.

**2.36**   The service organization has specified control objectives that it believes relate to assertions in the user organizations' financial statements and that are consistent with its contractual obligations. Table 2-3 indicates the control objectives specified by the service organization and the types of assertions in the user organizations' financial statements to which they relate.

## Table 2-3

### Examples of Assertions in User Organizations' Financial Statements and Related Service Organization Control Objectives *

| Assertions in User Organizations' Financial Statements | Control Objectives of the Service Organization |
|---|---|
| | Controls provide reasonable assurance that— |
| Completeness | Investment purchases and sales are recorded completely, accurately, and on a timely basis. |
| Valuation or allocation | Investment income is recorded accurately and timely. |
| Rights and obligations | Investment purchases and sales are recorded completely, accurately, and on a timely basis. |

* *Source:* Sample type 2 report for Example Trust Organization presented in Appendix A.

**2.37** The examples of control objectives presented in the preceding tables are not intended to be comprehensive or to suggest specific control objectives. They illustrate how a user organization's financial statement assertions may relate to a service organization's control objectives. Frequently, a financial statement assertion relates to more than one control objective, and a control objective relates to more than one financial statement assertion.

**2.38** Although the control objectives usually are specified by the service organization, they may be designated by an outside party, such as a regulatory agency or a user group. If the control objectives are specified by the service organization, they should be reasonable in the circumstances and consistent with the service organization's contractual obligations. If the control objectives are specified by an outside party, the outside party is responsible for their completeness and reasonableness.

**2.39** A service organization may design its service with the assumption that certain controls will be implemented by the user organizations. If such user organization controls are necessary to achieve certain control objectives, the service organization should describe the user organizations' responsibilities for those controls in its description of controls. Chapter 3 of this Guide, "Using Type 1 and Type 2 Reports," provides guidance to user auditors on complementary controls at user organizations, and Chapter 4 of this Guide, "Performing a Service Auditor's Engagement," gives guidance to service auditors on complementary controls at user organizations.

**2.40** Most service organizations depend primarily on computer processing to perform contracted services. Although a service organization may have some manual controls in place, it is often impractical for a service organization to implement sufficient manual controls to ensure accurate and timely computer processing. The service organization's description of controls should include a description of the computer environment and the related general computer control objectives and controls. This description should address such topics as program change controls, controls that restrict access to programs and data, and controls that affect the processing of data, because such information usually is relevant to a user organization's internal control. Likewise, deficiencies in certain general computer controls can affect both the proper operation of programmed procedures as well as the effectiveness of certain manual controls. Should such deficiencies exist, the service organization should describe their existence and their effect on key programmed procedures and manual controls performed by the service organization or manual controls user organizations are expected to perform.

**2.41** A service organization's plans related to business continuity and contingency planning generally are of interest to the managements of user organizations. If a service organization wishes to describe its business continuity and contingency plans, such information may be included in section 4, "Other Information Provided by the Service Organization." Because plans are not controls, a service organization should not include in its description of controls (section 2 of the report) a control objective that addresses business continuity or contingency planning. For additional information on the service auditor's responsibility for such information, see Auditing Interpretation No. 4, "Responsibilities of Service Organizations and Service Auditors With Respect to Forward-Looking Information in a Service Organization's Description of Controls," of SAS No. 70, as amended (AU sec. 9324.35–.37).

# Information Provided by the Service Auditor

**2.42** This section of a type 1 or type 2 report generally contains the following elements:

- A description of the tests of the operating effectiveness of controls and the results of those tests (This section would be included only in a type 2 report.)
- Other information the service auditor may provide (This is an optional section in both type 1 and type 2 reports.)

## The Description of Tests of the Operating Effectiveness of Controls and the Results of Those Tests

**2.43** Although the format of the description of the service auditor's procedures is flexible, it should provide an indication of the nature, timing, extent, and results of the tests of the operating effectiveness of controls that relate to specified control objectives. SAS No. 70, as amended, does not require that a service auditor describe tests of the control environment, risk assessment, monitoring, or information and communication. However, if a service auditor determines that describing tests of these components may be useful to user auditors, the service auditor may include such tests in the description of tests.

**2.44** In preparing the description of the tests of operating effectiveness, the service auditor should consider the extent of detail user auditors will need to determine the effect of such tests on their assessments of control risk. The description need not be a duplication of the service auditor's detailed audit program, which in some cases would make the report too voluminous for user auditors and would provide more than the required level of detail. However, the description should provide user auditors with enough information to determine whether control risk may be assessed below the maximum for certain financial statement assertions affected by the service organization's processing.

**2.45**   Although there is no single format for presenting a description of tests of operating effectiveness, the following elements should be included in the description:

- The controls that were tested.
- The control objectives the controls were intended to achieve.
- An indication of the nature, timing, extent, and results of the tests applied in sufficient detail to enable user auditors to determine the effect of such tests on their assessments of control risk. Detailed guidance about the content of this section is presented in Chapter 4, and examples of descriptions of tests of operating effectiveness are presented in the examples in paragraphs 4.49 through 4.94 and in Appendix A.

## Other Information a Service Auditor May Provide

**2.46**   In type 1 or type 2 reports, a service auditor may provide other information that may be useful to user organizations and their auditors. This information ordinarily would be included in section 3 of a type 1 or type 2 report, "Information Provided by the Service Auditor." Such information might more fully describe the objectives of a service auditor's engagement or might provide information relating to regulatory requirements.

**2.47**   A service auditor also may provide recommendations for improving the service organization's controls. These recommendations may be presented in a separate communication to the service organization or in section 3 of the document.

## Other Information Provided by the Service Organization

**2.48**   A service organization may wish to present other information in a separate section of a type 1 or type 2 report that is not a part of the description of controls and, consequently, is not covered by the service auditor's opinion. The service auditor should read such other information and consider applying by analogy the guidance in SAS No. 8, *Other Information in Documents Containing Audited Financial Statements* (AICPA, *Professional Standards*, vol. 1, AU sec. 550). Because this information is not a part of the description, the service auditor should include a paragraph in his or her report disclaiming an opinion on the other information provided by the service organization. Refer to paragraph 4.118 of this Guide for an example of such a disclaimer paragraph.

## Alternative Methods of Organizing Type 1 and Type 2 Reports

**2.49**   The method of organizing a type 1 or type 2 report presented in this chapter (that is, using four sections) is not meant to be a rigid standard. Accordingly, service organizations and service auditors may choose to organize their type 1 and type 2 reports in other ways. Examples 1 and 2 in Appendix A illustrate variations on the basic framework and are designed to eliminate redundancy in the document, as described in the following paragraphs.

**2.50**   In applying the framework presented in this chapter to a type 2 report, it is not necessary to list the controls and related control objectives in both the service organization's description of controls and in the service auditor's section of the document. To eliminate the redundancy that would result from repeating this information in both sections of the document, the Example Computer Service Organization type 2 report in Example 1 of Appendix A presents the controls and related control objectives only in the service auditor's section of the document. The table of contents of that type 2 report directs the reader to the service auditor's section of the document for a description of the control objectives and controls, and a paragraph in the service organization's description of controls indicates that the control objectives and related controls presented in the service auditor's section are the responsibility of the service organization and should be considered a part of the service organization's description of controls.

**2.51** In the Example Trust Organization type 2 report in Example 2 of Appendix A, the control objectives and controls along with the description of the tests of operating effectiveness, are presented in the service organization's section of the type 2 report. This is another method of presentation designed to avoid repetition of the control objectives and controls in both the service organization's section and the service auditor's section.

# Other Matters

## Engagements Involving Subservice Organizations

**2.52** Additional guidance on the form and content of a type 1 or type 2 report for situations in which a service organization uses another service organization (a subservice organization) to perform certain aspects of the processing performed for user organizations is presented in Chapter 5, "Service Organizations That Use Other Service Organizations."

## Certification of Computer Software

**2.53** A type 2 report is not intended to be a certification that computer software functions as designed or as asserted by the management of a service organization, but rather to provide information about the effectiveness of controls, which may include controls over the functioning of software. This can be illustrated by considering a situation in which a loan servicer uses a computer program to calculate interest. A type 1 or type 2 report would describe the controls that were designed to provide reasonable assurance that interest is calculated in conformity with the description, and a type 2 report would also provide information about the operating effectiveness of the controls that were tested. Such controls may be manual in nature (for example, recalculation of the interest accrual on a sample of loans) or automated (for example, controls embedded in the computer programs or controls over changes to and execution of the programs). A service auditor would identify and test the manual or automated controls to determine whether they provide reasonable assurance that interest is calculated in conformity with the description. However, the service auditor's report would not provide assurance that the software calculates interest accurately.

# Chapter 3

# Using Type 1 and Type 2 Reports*

**3.01**  This chapter provides guidance to user auditors on how and whether to use a given service auditor's report in an audit of a user organization's financial statements. It supplements Statement on Auditing Standards (SAS) No. 70, Service Organizations, as amended (AICPA, Professional Standards, vol. 1, AU sec. 324.18–.21), by describing factors a user auditor should consider when using a type 1 or type 2 report to plan the audit of a user organization's financial statements.

## Determining Whether to Use a Given Type 1 or Type 2 Report

**3.02**  In determining whether to use a given type 1 or type 2 report to plan the audit or to assess control risk, the user auditor should make inquiries about the professional reputation of the service auditor. SAS No. 70, as amended (AU sec. 324.18), provides additional guidance in this area.[1]

**3.03**  A user auditor should determine whether a given type 1 or type 2 report will meet his or her audit objectives. This topic is addressed in SAS No. 70, as amended (AU sec. 324.19). To make this determination, a user auditor should read the service auditor's report, the attached service organization's description of controls, and the information provided by the service auditor, which may include a description of tests of operating effectiveness and other information. A service auditor's report on a service organization's description of controls states whether the description is fairly presented; however, the report alone does not provide a user auditor with the understanding necessary to plan the audit.

**3.04**  In order for a user auditor to obtain a sufficient understanding of a user organization's internal control to plan the audit, he or she should consider the information presented in the type 1 or type 2 report, along with information about the user organization, to determine whether the user auditor has sufficient information to:

- Understand the aspects of the service organization's controls that may affect the processing of the user organization's transactions.

---

*  Refer to the Preface of this Guide for important information about the applicability of the professional standards to audits of issuers and non-issuers (see definitions in the Preface). As applicable, this chapter contains dual referencing to both the AICPA and the PCAOB professional standards. See the PCAOB web site at www.pcaobus.org for information about the effective date of PCAOB Auditing Standard No. 2 and related conforming amendments. For issuers, when performing an integrated audit of financial statements and internal control over financial reporting, refer to paragraphs B18-B29 of Appendix B, "Additional Performance Requirements and Directions; Extent-of-Testing Examples," in PCAOB Auditing Standard No. 2 regarding the use of service organizations. For additional guidance for issuers on the use of service organizations, see questions 24-26 and 28-29 of the PCAOB staff questions and answers on the PCAOB web site at www.pcaob.us.org/standards and questions 14 and 19 of the SEC frequently asked questions on management's report on internal control over financial reporting at www.sec.gov/info/accountants/controlfaq.1004.htm.

[1]  For audits of issuers, see question 26 of the PCAOB staff questions and answers at www.pcaobus.org/standards for guidance on whether a registered public accounting firm in the integrated audit of an issuer can obtain evidence from a service auditor's report issued by a non-registered public accounting firm.

- Understand the flow of significant transactions through the service organization. (The user auditor should use this information, along with information obtained from the user organization, to determine the points in the transaction flow where material misstatements in the user organization's financial statements could occur.)
- Determine whether the control objectives are relevant to the user organization's financial statement assertions.
- Determine whether the service organization's controls are suitably designed to prevent or detect processing errors that could result in material misstatements in the user organization's financial statements.

**3.05** The user auditor also should determine whether the service organization's description is as of a date that is appropriate for the user auditor's purposes.

**3.06** For purposes of assessing control risk below the maximum, as described in SAS No. 70, as amended (AU sec. 324.13), a user auditor should determine whether:

- A type 2 report provides adequate evidence of the nature, timing, extent, and results of the tests of operating effectiveness for the user auditor to determine whether he or she may assess control risk below the maximum for financial statement assertions affected by the service organization's processing.
- The timing of the tests of operating effectiveness performed by the service auditor is appropriate for the user auditor's purposes.
- The service auditor's report identifies results of tests (exceptions or other information) that could affect the user auditor's considerations. (Exceptions noted by the service auditor or a report modification in the service auditor's report do not automatically mean that the service auditor's report will not be useful in planning the audit of a user organization's financial statements or in assessing control risk.)

**3.07** If controls at a service organization are operating effectively, a user auditor may be able to assess control risk below the maximum for certain financial statement assertions affected by the service organization's service or processing, and reduce the substantive procedures performed for those assertions. To assess control risk below the maximum, a user auditor should evaluate the operating effectiveness of the relevant controls at the service organization in conjunction with the user organization's internal control. The user auditor also should consider whether the user organization has implemented complementary controls that are contemplated in the design of the service organization's controls and recommended in the service organization's description of controls. To determine whether the assessment of control risk may be reduced for assertions affected by the service organization's processing and whether the extent of substantive tests may be reduced, a user auditor should not only read the service auditor's report on operating effectiveness (the letter issued by the service auditor), but also should read and assess the testing performed and the results of the tests relevant to those assertions. The user auditor should consider the quality and quantity of the evidence provided by the report in determining whether it provides a sufficient basis for assessing control risk below the maximum for specified financial statement assertions. *In no case should a* user auditor consider only the service auditor's report (the letter issued by the service auditor) as the basis for reducing control risk below the maximum.

**3.08** If, after considering the user organization's internal control and other available information, a user auditor determines that the information in a type 1 or type 2 report does not meet his or her objectives, the user auditor may contact the service organization, through the user organization, to request that the service auditor perform agreed-upon procedures at the service organization, or the user auditor may perform such procedures. If the user auditor is still unsuccessful in gaining sufficient information to plan the audit, he or she should qualify his or her opinion on the financial statements because of a scope limitation.[2]

## Timing Considerations Related to Using a Service Organization's Description of Controls

**3.09** A service organization's description of controls is as of a specified date for both a type 1 and a type 2 report. Accordingly, the service auditor issues a report on whether the description presents fairly, in all material respects, the relevant aspects of the service organization's controls at a specified date. Such information may be used to plan the audit of a user organization's financial statements in the same way that an auditor's understanding of internal control at a specified date is used to plan the audit of the financial statements of an entity that does not use a service organization.

**3.10** A report on controls placed in operation that is as of a date outside the reporting period of a user organization may be useful in providing a user auditor with a preliminary understanding of the controls placed in operation at the service organization if the report is supplemented by additional current information from other sources. If the service organization's description is as of a date that precedes the beginning of the period under audit, the user auditor should consider updating the information in the description to determine whether there have been any changes in the service organization's controls relevant to the processing of the user organization's transactions. Procedures to update the information in a service auditor's report may include:

- Discussions with user-organization personnel who would be in a position to know about changes at the service organization.
- A review of current documentation and correspondence issued by the service organization.
- Discussions with service-organization personnel or with the service auditor.

**3.11** If the user auditor determines that there have been significant changes in the service organization's controls, the user auditor should attempt to gain an understanding of the changes and consider the effect of the changes on the audit.

---

[2] Paragraph 13.02 of the AICPA Audit and Accounting Guide *Employee Benefit Plans* indicates that historically the Department of Labor has rejected Form 5500, "Internal Revenue Service Annual Return/Report of Employee Benefit Plan," filings that contain either qualified opinions, adverse opinions, or disclaimers of opinion other than those issued in connection with a limited scope audit pursuant to 29 CFR 2520.103-8 or 12.

# The User Auditor's Consideration of Tests of Operating Effectiveness

**3.12** As indicated in Chapter 2, "Form and Content of Service Auditors' Reports," a type 2 report includes a description of tests of the operating effectiveness of certain controls that have been performed by the service auditor. If the user auditor intends to assess control risk below the maximum for certain financial statement assertions affected by the service organization's processing, the user auditor should determine whether the controls tested by the service auditor are relevant to the assertions in the user organization's financial statements. For tests of controls that are relevant, the user auditor should consider whether the nature, timing, extent, and results of the tests, in conjunction with the service auditor's report on the operating effectiveness of the controls, provide appropriate evidence to support the assessed level of control risk.

**3.13** In evaluating the tests of operating effectiveness, the user auditor should keep in mind that the shorter the period covered by a specific test and the longer the time elapsed since the performance of the test, the less support for control risk reduction the test may provide. For example, a report on a six-month testing period that covers only one or two months of the user organization's financial reporting period offers less support for control risk reduction than a report in which the testing covers six months of the user organization's financial reporting period. If the service auditor's testing period is completely outside the user organization's financial reporting period, the user auditor should not rely on such tests as support for control risk reduction because they do not provide current audit period evidence of the effectiveness of the controls, unless other procedures such as those described in the following paragraphs of SAS No. 55, *Consideration of Internal Control in a Financial Statement Audit,* as amended (AICPA, *Professional Standards,* vol. 1, AU sec. 319.97 and .98), are performed.

> 97. Evidential matter about the effective design or operation of controls that was obtained in prior audits may be considered by the auditor in assessing control risk in the current audit. To evaluate the use of such evidential matter for the current audit, the auditor should consider the significance of the assertion involved, the specific controls that were evaluated during the prior audits, the degree to which the effective design and operation of those controls were evaluated, the results of the tests of controls used to make those evaluations, and the evidential matter about design or operation that may result from substantive tests performed in the current audit. The auditor should also consider that the longer the time elapsed since the tests of controls were performed to obtain evidential matter about control risk, the less assurance they may provide.[3]
>
> 98. When considering evidential matter obtained from prior audits, the auditor should obtain evidential

---

[3] For issuers, paragraph 97 of SAS No. 55 has been amended by PCAOB Release 2004-008. When performing an integrated audit, refer to paragraphs 104–105 of PCAOB Auditing Standard No. 2 for discussion on the extent of tests of controls. (See AICPA, *PCAOB Standards and Related Rules,* AU sec. 319.97.)

matter in the current period about whether changes have occurred in internal control, including its policies, procedures and personnel, subsequent to the prior audits, as well as the nature and extent of any such changes. For example, in performing the prior audit, the auditor may have determined that an automated control was functioning as intended. The auditor should obtain evidence to determine whether changes to the automated control have been made that would affect its continued effective functioning. Consideration of evidential matter about these changes, together with the considerations in the preceding paragraph, may support either increasing or decreasing the evidential matter about the effectiveness of design and operation to be obtained in the current period.

## Complementary Controls That May Be Required at User Organizations

**3.14**   In certain circumstances, a service provided by the service organization may be designed with the assumption that certain controls will be implemented by the user organizations. For example, the service may be designed with the assumption that the user organizations will have controls in place for authorizing transactions before they are sent to the service organization for processing. If such complementary user organization controls are required to achieve the stated control objectives, the service organization should describe them in its description of controls. The user auditor should read the description of controls to determine whether complementary user organization controls are required and whether they are relevant to the service provided to that specific user organization. If they are relevant to the user organization, the user auditor should consider such information in planning the audit. Chapter 4, "Performing a Service Auditor's Engagement," provides guidance to the service auditor when complementary user organization controls are required.

## Reportable Conditions [4]

**3.15**   Reportable conditions are matters that come to the auditor's attention during a financial statement audit that, in the auditor's judgment, should be communicated to the audit committee or to individuals with a level of authority and responsibility equivalent to an audit committee because they represent significant deficiencies in the design or operation of the organization's internal control that could adversely affect the organization's ability to record, process, summarize, and report financial data consistent with management's assertions. Reportable conditions are defined in SAS No. 60, *Communication of Internal Control Related Matters Noted in an Audit* (AICPA, *Professional Standards*,

---

[4] For issuers, the term reportable conditions is replaced with the term significant deficiencies. SAS No. 60 has been superseded and its title changed to AU sec. 325, *Communications About Control Deficiencies in An Audit of Financial Statements*. For audits of financial statements only, SAS No. 60 has been superseded by certain paragraphs of PCAOB Release 2004-008. For integrated audits, SAS No. 60 has been superseded by paragraphs 207–214 of PCAOB Auditing Standard No. 2. (See AICPA, *PCAOB Standards and Related Rules*, AU sec. 325.)

vol. 1, AU sec. 325.02). When reading a type 1 or type 2 report, a user auditor may become aware of situations at the service organization that constitute reportable conditions for the user organization. Such situations may relate to the design or the operating effectiveness of the service organization's controls. In such circumstances, the user auditor should follow the guidance in SAS No. 60.

## Uncorrected Errors at the Service Organization

**3.16**   In the course of providing its services, a service organization may make errors that, if uncorrected, could affect one or more user organizations. Management of the service organization should report any uncorrected errors that are other than clearly inconsequential to the affected user organizations.

**3.17**   In performing the audit of a user organization, the user auditor should ask the user organization's management whether the service organization has reported any uncorrected errors to the user organization and should evaluate whether such errors will affect the nature, timing, and extent of his or her audit procedures. In certain instances, the user auditor may need to obtain additional information to make this evaluation and should consider contacting the service organization and the service auditor to obtain the necessary information.

# Chapter 4
# Performing a Service Auditor's Engagement[*]

**4.01** This chapter describes the responsibilities of the service organization and the service auditor in a service auditor's engagement. It also describes the procedures that should be performed in a service auditor's engagement and provides detailed reporting guidance for various situations that might arise in a type 1 or type 2 engagement.

**4.02** A service auditor's engagement consists of examining the service organization's description of controls to determine whether:

- It presents fairly, in all material respects, the relevant aspects of the service organization's controls that had been placed in operation as of a specified date.

- The controls were suitably designed to provide reasonable assurance that the specified control objectives would be achieved if those controls were complied with satisfactorily.

**4.03** In a type 2 engagement, the service auditor examines the service organization's description to achieve the two objectives described in the previous paragraph and also performs tests of certain controls to determine whether they were operating with sufficient effectiveness to provide reasonable, but not absolute, assurance that the related control objectives were achieved during the period specified.

**4.04** Statement on Auditing Standards (SAS) No. 70, *Service Organizations*, as amended (AICPA, *Professional Standards*, vol. 1, AU sec. 324.22–.56), describes the responsibilities of service auditors in reporting on controls placed in operation (type 1 engagements) and in reporting on controls placed in operation and tests of operating effectiveness (type 2 engagements).

## Responsibilities of the Service Organization

**4.05** In a service auditor's engagement, the service organization and the service auditor each have specific responsibilities. The service organization is responsible for preparing the description of controls. The service auditor may assist the service organization in preparing the description; however, the representations in the description are the responsibility of the service organization's management.

**4.06** The service organization is responsible for determining which services, business units, functional areas, or applications the service auditor will be engaged to report on, and for providing this information in its description. The service organization is responsible for the completeness, accuracy, and method of presentation of the description of controls, and is also responsible for specifying the control objectives, unless they are established by a third party.

---

[*] Refer to the Preface of this Guide for important information about the applicability of the professional standards to audits of issuers and non-issuers (see definitions in the Preface). As applicable, this chapter contains dual referencing to both the AICPA and the PCAOB's professional standards. See the PCAOB web site at www.pcaobus.org for information about the effective date of PCAOB Auditing Standard No. 2 and related conforming amendments.

**4.07**  As described in paragraph 2.19 of this Guide, the service organization also is responsible for describing any changes in controls since the later of the date of the last report or within the last 12 months. If the service auditor identifies any deficiencies in controls or changes in controls that have not been included in the service organization's description, or identifies other conditions that represent a significant deficiency in the design or operation of the service organization's controls, these changes or conditions should be disclosed as described in paragraphs 4.108 and 4.109 of this Guide.

**4.08**  The service organization determines whether the service auditor will perform a type 1 or type 2 engagement. In a type 2 engagement, the service organization specifies which control objectives will be tested for operating effectiveness and may engage a service auditor to test all of the control objectives identified in the description or a subset of the control objectives. Other responsibilities of the service organization include:

- Providing the service auditor with access to appropriate service organization resources, such as service organization personnel, systems documentation, contracts, and minutes of oversight committee meetings.

- Disclosing to the service auditor any significant changes in controls that have occurred since the service organization's last examination, or within the last 12 months if the service organization has not previously issued a service auditor's report.

- Disclosing to the service auditor and the affected user organizations any illegal acts, fraud, or uncorrected errors attributable to the service organization's management or employees that may affect one or more user organizations.

- Disclosing to the service auditor any relevant design deficiencies in controls of which it is aware, including those for which management believes the cost of corrective action may exceed the benefits.

- In a type 2 engagement, disclosing to the service auditor all instances of which it is aware when controls have not operated with sufficient effectiveness to achieve the specified control objectives.

- Providing the service auditor with a letter of representations.

**4.09**  The service organization should ensure that the description provides sufficient information, within the scope of the examination, for user auditors to obtain an understanding of the service organization's controls that may be relevant to the internal control of the user organizations. Chapter 2, "Form and Content of Service Auditors' Reports," provides guidance on the form and content of the service organization's description of controls.

# Responsibilities of the Service Auditor

## Procedures to Report on the Fairness of the Presentation of the Service Organization's Description of Controls

**4.10**  The service auditor should read the description of controls to gain an understanding of the representations made by management in the description. After reading the description, the service auditor should perform procedures to determine whether the description presents fairly, in all material respects, the relevant aspects of the service organization's controls that had been placed in operation. Service organization controls are considered *relevant* to user organizations if they represent or affect a user organization's internal control as it relates to an audit of financial statements. Service organization controls may represent or affect a user organization's control environment, risk assessment, control activities, information and communication, or monitoring components of internal control. The term *placed in operation* means that the controls have been implemented or put into practice, as opposed to existing only on paper. Placed in operation does not imply that the controls are suitably designed or operating with sufficient effectiveness to achieve control objectives.

**4.11** To determine whether the description is fairly presented, the service auditor should gain an understanding of the service provided by the service organization. Procedures to gain this understanding may include the following:

- Discussion with management and other service organization personnel
- Review of standard contracts with user organizations to gain an understanding of the service organization's contractual obligations
- Observation of the procedures performed by service organization personnel
- Review of service organization policy and procedure manuals and other systems documentation, for example, flowcharts and narratives
- Walk-through of selected transactions and controls[1]
- Determining who the user organizations are and how the services provided by the service organization are likely to affect the user organizations, for example, the predominant type(s) of user organizations, and whether user organizations are regulated by governmental agencies

**4.12** The service auditor should then compare his or her understanding of the service provided to user organizations with representations in the description to determine whether the service organization's description is fairly stated. The description is considered fairly stated if it describes controls in a manner that does not omit or distort information that may affect user auditors' decisions in planning the audit of the user organizations' financial statements and in assessing control risk.

**4.13** The service auditor should determine whether the description addresses all of the major aspects of the processing (within the scope of the engagement) that may be relevant to user auditors in planning the audit. There may be aspects of the services performed by the service organization that the user organizations may assume are within the scope of the engagement that may or may not be included in the scope of the engagement. For example, a service organization may have formal or informal controls related to the conversion of new user organizations to the service organization's systems. The service organization's description may not include a description of its controls related to the conversion of new user organizations to the service organization's systems because

---

[1] When preparing the service auditor's report, service auditors should be aware that auditors of issuers may be relying on the service auditor's report to obtain sufficient evidence to achieve the objectives of a walkthrough at the service organization, when performing an audit of internal control over financial reporting. Question 29 of the PCAOB staff questions and answers provides guidance on whether an auditor should perform walkthroughs at the service organization and says that the auditor may determine that it is possible to obtain sufficient evidence to understand the process flow of transactions at a service organization through the service auditor's report. See question 29 of the PCAOB staff questions and answers at www.pcaobus.org/standards for further guidance.

the service organization may consider such controls to be outside the normal processing services provided to user organizations, and outside the scope of the engagement. To avoid misunderstanding by readers of the description, it may be desirable to state whether the description covers controls related to the conversion of new user organizations to the service organization's systems.

**4.14** The service auditor also should determine whether the description objectively describes what is taking place at the service organization and whether it contains significant omissions or inaccuracies. The description should not state or imply that controls are being performed if they are not. This can be exemplified by considering a situation in which a service organization provides two different loan processing applications: application A, for which the service organization maintains independent totals and performs reconciliations of transactions processed, and application B, for which such totals are not maintained and for which reconciliations are not performed. The service organization's description should clearly indicate the application(s) that are being described. If both applications are being described, the description should indicate the different levels of service provided. For the description to be fairly stated, the service organization should state that independent totals and reconciliations are performed for application A and should not state or imply that they are performed for application B.

**4.15** If the service organization's description omits or misstates information that is within the scope of the engagement and that the service auditor believes user auditors would need to plan the audit, the service auditor should discuss the matter with management of the service organization and should ask management to amend the description. If management does not amend the description by including the omitted information or correcting the misstated information, the service auditor should consider issuing a qualified or adverse opinion on whether the service organization's description of controls presents fairly, in all material respects, the relevant aspects of the service organization's controls. In such circumstances, the service auditor should add an explanatory paragraph to the service auditor's report, preceding the opinion paragraph (the first opinion paragraph in a type 2 report). An example of such a paragraph follows:

> The accompanying description states that Example Service Organization maintains independent totals and performs reconciliations of transactions processed. Inquiries of staff personnel and inspection of activities indicate that such procedures are applied in application A but are not applied in application B.

**4.16** In addition, the first sentence of the opinion paragraph (the first opinion paragraph in a type 2 report) would be modified as follows:

> In our opinion, except for the matter referred to in the preceding paragraph, the accompanying description of the aforementioned applications presents fairly, in all material respects, the relevant aspects of Example Service Organization's controls that had been placed in operation as of December 31, 20XX.

**4.17** For the description to be considered fairly presented, it should contain a complete set of control objectives. SAS No. 70, as amended (AU sec. 324.35 and .50), states that control objectives may be designated by the service organization or by outside parties, such as regulatory authorities, a user group, or others. If the control objectives are established by the service organization, they should be reasonable in the circumstances and consistent with the service organization's contractual obligations. A complete and reasonable set of control objectives should provide user auditors with a basis for determining the effect of the service organization's controls on user organizations' financial statement assertions.

**4.18** To enable the service auditor to identify the kinds of user-organization financial statement assertions that are likely to be affected by the controls at the service organization, the service auditor should obtain a general understanding of the nature of the user organizations and how they use the services provided. The service auditor should determine whether the control objectives specified by the service organization relate to such assertions. The service auditor cannot, however, be aware of all of the assertions in user organizations' financial statements that might be affected by the service organization's controls or how those controls might affect the financial statement assertions of each user organization. Chapter 2 contains examples of how a service organization's control objectives might relate to a user organization's financial statement assertions.

**4.19** If the service auditor determines that the control objectives are not complete and reasonable in the circumstances, he or she should discuss the matter with the service organization's management and request that management amend the description by adding the appropriate control objective(s). If the service organization's management does not amend the description to include the recommended control objective(s), the service auditor should add an explanatory paragraph to the service auditor's report identifying the omitted control objective(s). For example, if a service organization provides loan servicing to financial institutions and asserts that loan payments received are completely and accurately recorded, it should include a control objective in its description of controls such as the following:

> Controls provide reasonable assurance that loan payments received from user organizations are completely and accurately recorded.

**4.20** The following is an example of an explanatory paragraph that should be inserted before the opinion paragraph of the service auditor's report (the first opinion paragraph in a type 2 report) if the control objectives are incomplete:

> The accompanying description of controls does not include a control objective related to the complete and accurate recording of loan payments received by Example Service Organization. We believe that this control objective and the related controls that might achieve this control objective should be specified in the Service Organization's description of controls because they are relevant to user organizations.

**4.21** In addition, the first sentence of the opinion paragraph (the first opinion paragraph in a type 2 report) should be modified as follows:

> In our opinion, except for the matter referred to in the preceding paragraph, the accompanying description of the aforementioned application presents fairly, in all material respects, the relevant aspects of Example Service Organization's controls that had been placed in operation as of December 31, 20XX.

**4.22** Depending on the severity of the omission, the service auditor may consider issuing an adverse opinion on whether the service organization's description of controls presents fairly, in all material respects, the relevant aspects of the service organization's controls. In such circumstances, the first sentence of the opinion paragraph of the service auditor's report (the first opinion paragraph in a type 2 report) should be modified as follows:

> In our opinion, because of the omission discussed in the preceding paragraph, the accompanying description of the aforementioned application does not present fairly, in all material respects, the relevant aspects of Example Service Organization's controls that had been placed in operation as of December 31, 20XX.

**4.23** Although the service auditor may qualify his or her opinion on the fairness of the presentation of the description of controls, the omission would not necessarily affect the service auditor's opinion on the suitability of the design or operating effectiveness of the controls because those opinions relate only to control objectives that are included in the service organization's description. The service auditor cannot report or comment on the suitability of the design or operating effectiveness of controls intended to achieve control objectives that are not included in the service organization's description of controls. The service auditor is not responsible for identifying or testing the controls that might achieve the omitted control objective(s).

**4.24** The service auditor should ensure that the control objectives are objectively stated so that individuals having competence in and using the same or similar measurement criteria would arrive at reasonably similar conclusions about the possible achievement of the control objectives. For example, the following control objective ordinarily would be too subjective for evaluation:

> Controls affecting physical access to computer equipment, storage media, and program documentation are adequate.

**4.25** This control objective could be reworded as follows to meet the objectivity criteria described earlier:

> Controls provide reasonable assurance that physical access to computer equipment, storage media, and program documentation is limited to properly authorized individuals.

**4.26** If the service auditor determines that the control objectives do not meet the objectivity criteria described earlier, the service auditor should ask the service organization's management to reword the control objectives. If management of the service organization does not reword the control objectives, the service auditor should consider modifying his or her opinion on whether the service organization's description of controls presents fairly, in all material respects, the relevant aspects of the service organization's controls.

**4.27** In some situations, the service organization may include objectives that would not be considered relevant to user auditors for the purpose of planning the audit and assessing control risk, such as objectives addressing the efficiency of the service organization's operations or its plans for the future. If such objectives are not relevant and cannot be objectively measured, they should be moved to the section of a type 1 or type 2 report entitled "Other Information Provided by the Service Organization" and be excluded from the scope of the service auditor's examination. Reporting guidance for such situations is presented later in this chapter under the heading "Elements of the Service Organization's Description That Are Not Covered by the Service Auditor's Report."

**4.28** In certain circumstances, the control objectives may be specified by an outside party, such as a regulatory agency or a user group. In these situations, the service auditor need not determine whether the control objectives are reasonable in the circumstances, consistent with the service organization's contractual obligations, and relevant to the user organizations' financial statement assertions. If the control objectives are established by an outside party, the service auditor's responsibility is to determine whether the control objectives in the description conform to those specified by the outside party.

## Procedures to Report on the Suitability of Design of Controls to Achieve Specified Control Objectives

**4.29** From the viewpoint of a user auditor, a control is suitably designed if individually, or in combination with other controls, it is likely to prevent or detect material misstatements in specific financial statement assertions. From the viewpoint of a service auditor in the context of a service auditor's engagement, a control is suitably designed if individually, or in combination with other controls, it is likely to prevent or detect errors that could result in the nonachievement of specified control objectives when the described controls are complied with satisfactorily. To determine if controls are suitably designed to achieve specified control objectives, the service auditor should:

- Consider the linkage between the controls and the specified control objectives.
- Consider the ability of the controls to prevent or detect errors related to the control objectives.
- Perform procedures, such as inquiry of appropriate entity personnel, inspection of documents and reports, and observation of the application of specific controls, to determine whether they are suitably designed to achieve the specified control objectives. A service auditor may consider using flowcharts, questionnaires, or decision tables to facilitate his or her understanding of the design of the controls.

**4.30** After performing procedures such as those mentioned above, a service auditor may conclude that the controls are not suitably designed to achieve specified control objectives. For example, a service organization may identify the reconciliation of input to output as a control designed to achieve the control objective that all output is complete and accurate, but the organization may not have a control requiring follow-up of reconciling items and independent review of the reconciliations. The service auditor should consider this design deficiency in his or her overall assessment of the controls designed to achieve the control objective that all output is complete and accurate. The following is an example of an explanatory paragraph that should be added to the service auditor's report, preceding the opinion paragraph (the first opinion paragraph in a type 2 report) if the service auditor determines that controls are not suitably designed to achieve a specified control objective.

> As discussed in the accompanying description, Example Service Organization reconciles the listing of loan payments received with the output generated. The reconciliation procedures, however, do not include a control for follow-up on reconciling items and for independent review and approval of

the reconciliations. These deficiencies result in the controls not being suitably designed to achieve the control objective, "Controls provide reasonable assurance that all output is complete and accurate."

**4.31**    In such a situation, the opinion paragraph of the service auditor's report (the first opinion paragraph in a type 2 report) should be modified as follows:

> In our opinion, the accompanying description of the aforementioned application presents fairly, in all material respects, the relevant aspects of Example Service Organization's controls that had been placed in operation as of December 31, 20XX. Also, in our opinion, except for the matter described in the preceding paragraph, the controls, as described, are suitably designed to provide reasonable assurance that the specified control objectives would be achieved if the described controls were complied with satisfactorily.

## Procedures to Report on the Operating Effectiveness of Controls to Achieve Specified Control Objectives

**4.32**    In a type 2 engagement, the service auditor performs tests of controls to determine whether they were operating with sufficient effectiveness to achieve the related control objectives during a specified period. Operating effectiveness is concerned with how a control is applied, the consistency with which it is applied, and by whom it is applied. As previously stated, the service organization specifies which control objectives are to be tested and the service auditor determines which controls are necessary to achieve the control objectives specified by management. The service auditor may conclude that all or only a portion of the controls identified by management are necessary to achieve a control objective. The service auditor also determines the nature, timing, and extent of the tests to be performed to express his or her opinion on the operating effectiveness of the controls.

**4.33**    Procedures to test the operating effectiveness of the controls may include the following procedures, or a combination thereof:

- Inquiry of appropriate service organization personnel
- Inspection of documents, reports, or other data
- Observation of the application of the control
- Reperformance of the control

**4.34**    Some tests of controls provide more convincing evidence of the operating effectiveness of the controls than others do. Evidential matter obtained directly by the service auditor, such as through observation, provides greater assurance than evidential matter obtained indirectly or by inference, such as through inquiry. However, a service auditor should consider that a control that is being observed might not be performed in the same manner when the auditor is not present. Also, inquiry alone generally will not provide sufficient evidential matter to support a conclusion about the operating effectiveness of a specific control.

**4.35**    A service auditor should perform tests of relevant aspects of the control environment, risk assessment, and monitoring related to the service provided and assess their effectiveness in establishing, enhancing, or mitigating the effectiveness of specific controls. As relevant aspects of the control environment, risk assessment, and monitoring are judged to be less effective, more evidence of the operating effectiveness of the controls should be gathered to determine whether a control objective has been achieved. In some cases, deficiencies may be so pervasive that the service auditor will need to modify his or her opinion on the achievement of one or more control objectives. In a type 2 report, a service auditor may include a description of the nature, timing, and extent of the tests of the relevant aspects of the control environment, risk assessment, and monitoring in the section of the report that describes the service auditor's tests and results. Chapter 2, "Form and Content of Service Auditors' Reports," provides guidance on the features of a service organization's control environment, risk assessment, and monitoring that may affect the services provided to user organizations.

**4.36**  The nature, timing, and extent of the tests of operating effectiveness also are affected by the period covered by the report. Tests of operating effectiveness should provide evidence that will enable the service auditor to report on the entire period covered by the report. To be useful to user auditors, the report ordinarily should cover a minimum reporting period of six months. If the service auditor is engaged to report on a period of less than six months, he or she should describe the reasons for the shorter period in the service auditor's section of the report. Circumstances that might necessitate a report covering a period of less than six months include:

- Engagement of the service auditor close to the report issuance date in a situation where certain controls can be tested only through observation.

- A service organization, system, or application that has been in operation for less than six months.

- Significant system changes have occurred and it is not practicable either to (1) wait six months before issuing a report or (2) issue a report covering both the system before and after the changes.

**4.37**  Certain controls may not leave documentary evidence that can be tested at a later date. A service auditor may need to test the operating effectiveness of such controls at various times throughout the reporting period.

**4.38**  Situations may arise in which the service auditor's tests of operating effectiveness do not cover the same period for all control objectives. In such cases, the service auditor's report should disclose the applicable test periods.

**4.39**  Evidence from prior service auditor's engagements may also affect the nature, timing, and extent of the tests of operating effectiveness. To provide a basis for a reduction in testing, such evidential matter should be supplemented with evidential matter obtained during the current period to support the service auditor's conclusion that the relevant controls were operating effectively. Decisions about the degree of assurance that may be obtained from prior engagement evidence and about the additional evidential matter needed in the current period are affected by considerations such as the following.

- Conditions that could affect the operating effectiveness of the controls, such as:
  - A change in the nature of the transactions being processed
  - An increase in the volume of the transactions being processed

— An increase in the number of changes made to the procedures, the system, or the computer programs
— An increase in the number of user organizations
— A change in management's attitude or a reduction in supervision
— High turnover of employees
— An increase in the responsibilities or workloads of employees

- The effects of related controls and relevant aspects of the control environment, risk assessment, and monitoring that reinforce the continuing operating effectiveness of controls, such as:

— The existence of documented procedures manuals
— Close management supervision, including frequent communication and responsibility reporting
— Periodic reviews by internal auditors
— Effective general computer controls, such as program change controls

**4.40** The service auditor should determine whether there were changes in the controls subsequent to the previous engagement and should gather information about the nature and extent of such changes. If such changes are relatively minor, evidential matter obtained in prior audits may provide evidence for the current engagement and may consequently reduce, but not eliminate, the need for additional evidence in the current period. Conversely, changes may be so significant that evidential matter obtained in prior engagements may provide limited or no evidence of operating effectiveness for the current engagement.

**4.41** Readers of this Guide should refer to SAS No. 55, *Consideration of Internal Control in a Financial Statement Audit*, as amended (AICPA, *Professional Standards*, vol. 1, AU sec. 319.96–.99)[2] for guidance on the timeliness and the degree of assurance provided by evidential matter and should refer to SAS No. 39, *Audit Sampling* (AICPA, *Professional Standards*, vol. 1, AU sec. 350), for guidance when sampling is used in performing tests of operating effectiveness.

# Describing Tests of Operating Effectiveness and the Results of Those Tests

**4.42** SAS No. 70, as amended (AU sec. 324.44), specifies the elements that should be included in a description of tests of operating effectiveness. It states in part:

> The description should include the controls that were tested, the control objectives the controls were intended to achieve, the tests applied, and the results of the tests. The description should include an indication of the nature, timing, and extent of the tests, as well as sufficient detail to enable user auditors to determine the effect of such tests on user auditors' assessments of control risk. To the extent that the service

---

[2] For issuers, paragraph 97 of SAS No. 55 has been amended by PCAOB Release 2004-008. When performing an integrated audit, refer to paragraphs 104–105 of PCAOB Auditing Standard No. 2 for discussion on the extent of tests of controls. (See AICPA, *PCAOB Standards and Related Rules*, AU sec. 319.97.)

auditor identified causative factors for exceptions, determined the current status of corrective actions, or obtained other relevant qualitative information about exceptions noted, such information should be provided.

**4.43** Auditing Interpretation No. 1, "Describing Tests of Operating Effectiveness and the Results of Such Tests," of SAS No. 70, as amended (AICPA, *Professional Standards*, vol. 1, AU sec. 9324.01–.03), indicates that in all cases, for each control objective tested, the description of tests of operating effectiveness should include all of the elements listed in SAS No. 70, as amended (AU sec. 324.44), whether or not the service auditor concludes that the control objective has been achieved. The description should provide sufficient information to enable user auditors to assess control risk for financial statement assertions affected by the service organization. The description need not be a duplication of the service auditor's detailed audit program, which in some cases would make the report too voluminous for user auditors and would provide more than the required level of detail.

**4.44** The interpretation also indicates that in describing the nature, timing, and extent of the tests applied, the service auditor also should indicate whether the items tested represent a sample or all the items in the population, but need not indicate the size of the population, except as noted below. In describing the results of the tests, the service auditor should include exceptions and other information that in the service auditor's judgment could be relevant to user auditors. Such exceptions and other information should be included for each control objective, whether or not the service auditor concludes that the control objective has been achieved. When exceptions that could be relevant to user auditors are noted, the description also should include the following information:

- The size of the sample, if sampling has been used
- The number of exceptions noted
- The nature of the exceptions

**4.45** If the service auditor has identified causative factors for exceptions, determined the current status of corrective actions, or obtained other relevant qualitative information about exceptions noted, that information also should be provided.

**4.46** If no exceptions or other information that could be relevant to user auditors are identified by the tests, the service auditor should indicate that finding with remarks such as "no relevant exceptions noted," "no exceptions noted," or "controls operating as described."

## Examples of Descriptions of Tests of Operating Effectiveness and the Results of Those Tests

**4.47** The following examples illustrate situations in which a service auditor performs tests of the operating effectiveness of controls, evaluates the results of the tests, and determines what information to include in the description of the results of tests. In each situation, the rationale used by the service auditor in determining what information to include in the description of the results of tests is presented. It is assumed that in each situation other relevant controls and tests of operating effectiveness also would be described. As in all aspects of the engagement, a service auditor should use his or her judgment in determining what information to include in the results of tests.

**4.48** In Examples 1 and 2 that follow, the service auditor is performing tests of the operating effectiveness of controls at a bank trust organization. Some of the services performed by the trust organization include purchasing and selling securities for user organizations upon their specific authorization, recording such transactions, and maintaining book-entry records of the securities owned by the user organizations.

## Example 1

**4.49** *Control objective specified by the service organization.* Controls provide reasonable assurance that purchases of securities are authorized.

**4.50** *Control described by the service organization for this objective.* Securities are purchased for user organizations only after the service organization receives a security purchase authorization form signed by an employee of the user organization who has been specifically designated by the user organization to authorize purchases.

**4.51** *Tests of operating effectiveness performed by the service auditor.* The service auditor inspected a sample of $n$ [3] security purchase authorization forms for an appropriate user employee signature.

**4.52** *Results of tests.* One of the $n$ security purchase authorization forms did not have an appropriate user employee signature.

**4.53** *Reporting test results.* The service auditor concluded that user organizations and user auditors may be relying on the operating effectiveness of the control that requires appropriate user employee signatures on security purchase authorization forms to ensure that purchases of securities are properly authorized by the user organizations. The service auditor also concluded that information about the potential for unauthorized security purchases could be relevant to user auditors' assessments of control risk; accordingly, the service auditor concluded that this information would be included in the results of tests.

## Example 2

**4.54** *Control objective specified by the service organization.* Controls provide reasonable assurance that purchases of securities are authorized.

**4.55** *Controls described by the service organization for this objective.* Securities are purchased for user organizations only after the service organization receives authorization from the user organization. The service organization obtains such authorization through one of the following procedures: (1) receiving a security purchase authorization form signed by an employee of the user organization who has been designated by the user organization to authorize purchases or (2) if a form is submitted without an appropriate authorizing signature, performing a callback procedure in which a telephone call is placed to a specifically designated user employee to obtain verbal authorization, and maintaining a record, such as a tape recording, of such authorization.

---

[3] The sample size in each of the examples in this section is denoted by the letter $n$. Actual sample sizes would be determined by the service auditor.

**4.56** *Tests of operating effectiveness performed by the service auditor.* The service auditor inspected a sample of $n$ security purchase authorization forms for evidence of an appropriate user employee signature.

**4.57** *Results of tests.* One of the $n$ security purchase authorization forms did not have an appropriate user signature. For the form without the signature, the service auditor inspected the callback documentation and determined that the callback procedure had been performed.

**4.58** *Reporting test results.* The service auditor concluded that the results of tests did not constitute an exception. Although the user signature was missing from one of the security purchase authorization forms, the callback procedure identified in the service organization's description had been performed. The results of the tests performed provided evidence that the identified controls were operating effectively to ensure that an appropriately authorized employee of the user organization had authorized the purchase. Unlike the situation described in Example 1, the missing signature does not constitute an exception in this case because (1) the control described is to obtain a signature or, in the absence of a signature, to perform the callback procedure and (2) the callback procedure was performed and documented.

**4.59** The service auditor also considered whether it would be relevant to user auditors that one of the $n$ items tested was authorized by a callback procedure rather than a signature. The service auditor concluded that this information would not be relevant to user auditors; accordingly, the service auditor concluded that the information about the missing signature would not be included in the results of tests. *If the service auditor had concluded that the number of items tested for which signatures were missing and callback procedures had been performed could have been relevant to user auditors, the service auditor would have reported such information in the results of tests.*

**4.60** In Examples 3 and 4, the service auditor is performing tests of the operating effectiveness of controls at a data processing service organization that processes transactions for user organizations.

## Example 3

**4.61** *Control objective specified by the service organization.* Controls provide reasonable assurance that changes to application software are authorized, tested, and approved.

**4.62** *Control described by the service organization for this objective.* The programming manager is required to sign (1) a program change form to authorize the change, and (2) the results of testing to indicate that the change has been made as authorized.

**4.63** *Tests of operating effectiveness performed by the service auditor.* For a sample of $n$ program changes, the service auditor inspected the related program change forms and results of testing for the programming manager's signature.

**4.64** *Results of tests.* For one of the $n$ changes, the programming manager's signature was missing from the program change form but was present on the results of testing.

**4.65** *Reporting test results.* The service auditor concluded that the programming manager's signature on the results of testing provided evidence that the programming manager had also authorized the change. The service auditor concluded that the absence of the programming manager's signature on the program change form would not be relevant to user auditors; accordingly, the service auditor concluded that information about the missing signature would not be included in the results of tests.

## Example 4

**4.66** *Control objective specified by the service organization.* Controls provide reasonable assurance that changes to application software are authorized, tested, and approved.

**4.67** *Control described by the service organization for this objective.* The programming manager is required to sign (1) the program change form to authorize the change and (2) the results of testing to indicate that the change has been made as authorized.

**4.68** *Tests of operating effectiveness performed by the service auditor.* For a sample of $n$ program changes, the service auditor inspected the related program change forms and results of testing for the programming manager's signatures.

**4.69** *Results of tests.* For one of the $n$ changes, the programming manager's signature was missing from the results of testing. The programming manager's signature was present on all program change forms.

**4.70** *Reporting test results.* The service auditor concluded that the absence of the programming manager's signature on the results of testing could result in an increased risk that an authorized change could be incorrectly made. Because this could affect user auditors' assessments of control risk for assertions affected by the computer processing, the service auditor concluded that information about the missing signature would be included in the results of tests.

**4.71** In Examples 5 and 6, the service auditor is performing tests of the operating effectiveness of controls that prevent unauthorized access to programs and data at a data processing service organization.

## Example 5

**4.72** *Control objective specified by the service organization.* Controls provide reasonable assurance that access to programs and data is restricted to appropriately authorized individuals.

**4.73** *Control described by the service organization for this objective.* The service organization uses software to control access to programs and data. User organizations provide the service organization with an appropriately signed form to change a user employee's access to the system. The service organization makes the change within one business day of notification from the user organization.

**4.74** *User control considerations.* User organizations are responsible for notifying the service organization when there is a need to change a user employee's access privileges.

**4.75** *Tests of operating effectiveness performed by the service auditor.* The service auditor inspected a sample of $n$ forms requesting termination of user access for specified employees to determine whether and when access for those employees had been terminated. The service auditor also inspected customer service logs of user organization complaints.

**4.76** *Results of tests.* Of the *n* forms tested, one user employee retained access to the system for four business days after the request for termination of access had been received.

**4.77** *Reporting test results.* The significance of this exception could be evaluated by user auditors only in the context of other factors at the user organization, for example, the number of employees with access to the system for whom access had been terminated, the reasons for termination of access, the nature of the employees' access, and the existence of other relevant controls at the user organizations. Accordingly, the service auditor concluded that this information would be included in the results of tests.

## Example 6

**4.78** *Control objective specified by the service organization.* Controls provide reasonable assurance that access to programs and data is restricted to appropriately authorized individuals.

**4.79** *Control described by the service organization for this objective.* The service organization uses software to control access to programs and data. User organizations provide the service organization with an appropriately signed form to change a user employee's access to the system. The service organization makes the change within one business day of notification from the user organization.

**4.80** *User control considerations.* User organizations are responsible for notifying the service organization when there is a need to change a user employee's access privileges.

**4.81** *Tests of operating effectiveness performed by the service auditor.* The service auditor inspected a sample of *n* forms requesting termination of user access for specified employees to determine whether and when the employees' access to the system had been terminated. The service auditor also inspected customer service logs of user organization complaints.

**4.82** *Results of tests.* The service auditor noted three instances when user organizations complained that their employees' access had not been terminated within one business day of the employees' termination. The service auditor inspected the requests to change user employee access forms for these instances and determined that the user organizations had submitted the requests from one to three weeks after the employees had been terminated. Correspondence indicated that the service organization had discussed these instances with the affected user organizations.

**4.83** *Reporting test results.* The service auditor concluded that the instances noted resulted from the user organizations' failures to properly execute controls that were their responsibility (as described in the user control considerations section of the description of controls), and were not exceptions in the service organization's application of controls. Because the description of controls clearly indicates the user organizations' responsibilities, and because the items noted had been communicated to the affected user organizations, the service auditor concluded that information about the complaints of delayed termination of employees' access to the system would not be included in the results of tests. *If, after considering the specific facts and circumstances in the situation, the service auditor concluded that information about the user organizations' complaints of delayed termination of employee access to the system* *could be relevant to user auditors, that information would be included in the results of tests.*

**4.84** In Examples 7 and 8, the service auditor is performing tests of the operating effectiveness of controls at a trust organization. One of the services performed by the trust organization is recording transactions for user organizations.

## Example 7

**4.85** *Control objective specified by the service organization.* Controls provide reasonable assurance that security purchase and sale transactions are recorded at the appropriate amounts and in the appropriate periods.

**4.86** *Control described by the service organization for this objective.* Reconciliations are performed daily and reconciling items are identified and resolved within 10 days and before the issuance of customer statements.

**4.87** *Tests of operating effectiveness performed by the service auditor.* The service auditor inspected a sample of *n* reconciliations covering the test period.

**4.88** *Results of tests.* Reconciliations are performed daily and reconciling items are identified and resolved within 10 days and before the issuance of customer statements. Reconciling items for the reconciliations inspected appeared to result from normal processing and ranged from a few cents to several thousand dollars.

**4.89** *Reporting test results.* The service auditor concluded that the results of tests provide evidence that the identified controls were operating effectively. The service auditor also concluded that the reconciling items in the reconciliations inspected resulted from normal processing and were being appropriately identified and resolved. Accordingly, the service auditor indicated that no exceptions had been noted in the tests of operating effectiveness. *If the service auditor had concluded that information about the reconciling items or the results of tests could be relevant to user auditors, that information would be included in the description of tests of operating effectiveness. For example, the service auditor might wish to communicate that the number and age of the reconciling items appeared reasonable and within the service organization's guidelines. (The sample service auditor's report for Example Trust Organization, presented in Example 2 of Appendix A, illustrates this point.)*

## Example 8

**4.90** *Control objective specified by the service organization.* Controls provide reasonable assurance that security purchase and sale transactions are recorded at the appropriate amounts and in the appropriate periods.

**4.91** *Controls described by the service organization for this objective.* Reconciliations are performed daily and reconciling items are identified and resolved within 10 days and before the issuance of customer statements.

**4.92** *Tests of operating effectiveness performed by the service auditor.* The service auditor inspected a sample of *n* reconciliations covering the test period.

**4.93** *Results of tests.* Reconciling items ranged from a few cents to several thousand dollars. Reconciling items were identified timely but were not always resolved within the 10-day period and before the issuance of customer statements.

**4.94** *Reporting test results.* The service auditor concluded that the service organization's failure to consistently resolve all reconciling items within the required period could affect user auditors' assessments of whether transactions are completely and accurately reflected in customers' statements. Accordingly, the service auditor concluded that this information would be included in the results of tests.

# Reporting When Controls Are Not Operating Effectively

**4.95** A service auditor should evaluate the results of the tests of operating effectiveness and the significance of any exceptions noted. The service auditor may conclude that specified control objectives have been achieved even if exceptions have been noted and reported. If the service auditor determines that controls are not operating with sufficient effectiveness to achieve specified control objectives, the service auditor should report those conditions in an explanatory paragraph of the service auditor's report preceding the paragraph expressing an opinion on operating effectiveness. An example of such a paragraph follows:

> The Service Organization states in its description of controls that it has controls in place to reconcile loan payments received with the output generated, to follow up on reconciling items, and to independently review the reconciliation procedures. Our tests of operating effectiveness noted that significant reconciling items were not being resolved on a timely basis in accordance with the Service Organization's policy. This resulted in the nonachievement of the control objective "Controls provide reasonable assurance that loan payments received are properly recorded."

**4.96** In addition, the first sentence of the paragraph expressing an opinion on operating effectiveness should be modified as follows:

> In our opinion, except for the matter described in the preceding paragraph, the controls that were tested, as described in section 3, were operating with sufficient effectiveness to provide reasonable, but not absolute, assurance that the control objectives specified in section 3 were achieved during the period from January 1, 20XX, to December 31, 20XX.

# Additional Comments Related to Type 2 Engagements

**4.97** As previously stated in this chapter, in a type 2 engagement the service auditor performs procedures to determine whether (1) the description presents fairly the controls that have been placed in operation as of a specified date, (2) the controls were suitably designed to achieve specified control objectives, and (3) the controls were operating with sufficient effectiveness to provide reasonable assurance that the control objectives were achieved for the specified period. The nature and objectives of the tests performed to evaluate the fairness of the presentation of the description are different from those performed to evaluate the operating effectiveness of the controls.

**4.98** For instance, the description of controls for Example Computer Service Organization presented in Example 1 of Appendix A would ordinarily describe the method of calculating the interest on savings account balances and the controls that provide reasonable assurance that interest is calculated in conformity with the description (see control objective 10 in Example 1 of Appendix A). To determine whether the description of the calculation of interest is fairly presented, the service auditor would perform procedures, such as walk-throughs or reperformance of the calculations, to determine whether the calculation, as described, had been placed in operation. Because the interest calculations are dependent on the general computer controls, the service auditor also would perform procedures to determine whether the service organization's description of the general computer controls is fairly stated.

**4.99**  The objective of tests of the operating effectiveness of controls is to determine how the described controls are applied, the consistency with which they are applied, and by whom they are applied. In Example Computer Service Organization's description of tests of operating effectiveness, the tests of the operating effectiveness of the controls that provide reasonable assurance that interest is calculated in conformity with the description, are limited to tests of the general computer controls because the service organization relies on the computer to calculate interest in conformity with the description. The service auditor generally would not indicate that the only test of operating effectiveness performed was to recalculate interest.

# Other Matters Related to Performing a Service Auditor's Engagement

## Complementary Controls at User Organizations

**4.100**  In performing his or her procedures and in considering the service organization's description of controls, it may become evident to the service auditor that the service was designed with the assumption that certain controls would be implemented by user organizations. Such controls are called *complementary user organization controls*. Examples of complementary user organization controls include:

- Controls at the user organization over passwords needed to access the service organization's applications through computer terminals.
- Controls at the user organization to ensure that all input sent to the service organization is complete, accurate, and authorized.
- Controls at the user organization to ensure that all required output is received from the service organization and reconciled to the input sent to the service organization.

**4.101**  Such required complementary user organization controls should be delineated in the service organization's description of controls. If the service organization's description does not identify the complementary user organization controls, the service auditor should request that the management of the service organization amend its description of controls to include that information. If management does not amend the description, the service auditor should consider adding an explanatory paragraph to the report that describes the required complementary user organization controls and should consider qualifying his or her opinion on the fairness of the presentation of the description.

**4.102**  In certain situations, the application of user organization controls may be necessary to achieve a specified control objective. A service organization that provides payroll services to user organizations and receives input payroll transactions from user organizations via remote terminals might establish the following control objective.

> Controls provide reasonable assurance that all input to the application is authorized.

**4.103** This control objective could not be achieved without the implementation of input controls at the user organizations because transaction authorization rests with the user organizations. The service organization only can be responsible for ensuring that input transactions are received from sources identified as authorized by the user organizations. Accordingly, if the control objective were "Controls provide reasonable assurance that all input is received from authorized sources," the control objective could be achieved without controls at the user organizations.

**4.104** If the application of user organization controls is necessary to achieve a stated control objective, the service auditor should add the phrase "and user organizations applied the controls contemplated in the design of service organization controls" following the words "complied with satisfactorily" in the scope and opinion paragraphs of the service auditor's report.

## Other Design Deficiencies Irrespective of Specified Control Objectives

**4.105** Within the scope of the examination, the service auditor should consider whether any other information, irrespective of specified control objectives, has come to his or her attention that causes him or her to conclude (1) that design deficiencies exist that could adversely affect the ability of the service organization to record, process, summarize, or report financial data to user organizations without error, and (2) that user organizations would not generally be expected to have controls in place to mitigate such design deficiencies. However, a service auditor is not required to search for such deficiencies. If deficiencies are identified and the service organization does not describe them in its description of controls, the service auditor should request that management amend the description. If management does not amend the description, the service auditor should:

- Describe such deficiencies in a separate explanatory paragraph of his or her report, preceding the paragraph expressing an opinion on fair presentation.

- Qualify his or her opinion on the fairness of the presentation of the description because the description is not fairly stated as of the date of the description.

**4.106** SAS No. 70, as amended (AU sec. 324.32), addresses design deficiencies that could adversely affect processing *during the period covered by the service auditor's examination*. It does not apply to design deficiencies that potentially could affect processing *in future periods*. For example, if computer programs are correctly processing data during the period covered by the service auditor's examination, and such design deficiencies currently do not affect user organizations' abilities to record, process, summarize, or report financial data, the service auditor would not be required to report such design deficiencies in his or her report, based on the requirements in SAS No. 70, as amended

(AU sec. 324.32). However, if a service auditor becomes aware of design deficiencies at the service organization that potentially could affect the processing of user organizations' transactions in future periods, the service auditor, in his or her judgment, may choose to communicate this information to the service organization's management and may consider advising management to disclose this information and its plans for correcting the design deficiencies in a section of the service auditor's document titled "Other Information Provided by the Service Organization." If the service organization includes information about such design deficiencies in that section of the document, the service auditor should read the information and consider the guidance in SAS No. 8, *Other Information in Documents Containing Audited Financial Statements* (AICPA, *Professional Standards*, vol. 1, AU sec. 550). In addition, the service auditor should include a paragraph in his or her report disclaiming an opinion on the information provided by the service organization. A service auditor also may consider communicating information about such design deficiencies in the section of the service auditor's document titled "Other Information Provided by the Service Auditor."

## Changes in the Service Organization's Controls

**4.107** Although a service organization's description of controls is as of a specified date, the service auditor should inquire about changes in the service organization's controls. If the service auditor believes that the changes would be considered significant by user auditors, those changes should be described in the service organization's description of controls. Generally, changes that occurred more than 12 months before the date being reported on would not be considered significant because they generally would not affect user auditors' considerations.

**4.108** SAS No. 70, as amended (AU sec. 324.28 and .43), presents examples of changes in the service organization's controls that might be considered significant to user auditors. Such changes might include the following:

- Procedural changes made to accommodate provisions of a new Financial Accounting Standards Board (FASB) Statement of Financial Accounting Standards or provisions of new regulatory requirements
- Major changes in an application to permit online processing or to permit Internet access
- Major changes in an application to automate certain manual procedures
- Procedural changes to eliminate previously identified deficiencies
- Implementation of a single sign-on process
- Changes affecting the control environment, risk assessment, or monitoring resulting from a change in service organization ownership

**4.109** If the service organization does not include the changes in its description of controls, the service auditor should request that management amend the description. If management does not amend the description, the service auditor should describe the changes in a separate explanatory paragraph of his or her report, preceding the paragraph expressing an opinion on fair presentation of the description. The omission of the information about changes in the service organization's controls does not, however, warrant a qualification of the opinion on the fairness of presentation of the description because the description is fairly stated as of the date of the description. The explanatory paragraph should include the following:

- A description of the previous control(s)
- A description of the current control(s)
- An indication of when the change occurred

**4.110** The following is an example of an explanatory paragraph that would be added to the service auditor's report before the opinion paragraph (the first opinion paragraph in a type 2 report) if disclosure about a significant change had not been included in the service organization's description of controls:

> The accompanying description states that the quality assurance group reviews a random sample of work performed by input clerks to determine the degree of compliance with the organization's input standards. Inquiries of staff personnel indicate that this control was first implemented on July 1, 20XX.

## Changes in the Control Objectives to Be Tested

**4.111** At any time during the engagement, the service organization may change which control objectives will be tested for operating effectiveness. However, if the service auditor believes that any change in the control objectives to be tested would be considered significant by user organizations and their auditors, or if the service auditor considers conditions that come to his or her attention to represent a significant deficiency in the design or operation of the service organization's controls, these changes or conditions should be disclosed in the description of the service organization's controls (SAS No. 70, as amended [AU sec. 324.32 for Type 1 engagements and AU sec. 324.47 for Type 2 engagements]). Before changing the type of engagement or the control objectives to be tested, the service organization should consider the effect these changes may have on the user organizations and the user auditors.

## Service Auditor's Recommendations for Improving Controls

**4.112** Although it is not the objective of a service auditor's engagement, a service auditor may develop recommendations to improve a service organization's controls. The service auditor and the service organization should agree on how these recommendations will be communicated. In some situations, the service organization's management may request that the service auditor present this information in the service auditor's section of the report. In other situations, management may request that the service auditor include this information in a separate communication. Management's responses to such recommendations also may be included.

## Uncorrected Errors, Fraud, or Illegal Acts at a Service Organization[4]

**4.113** The terms *errors* and *fraud* are defined in SAS No. 47, *Audit Risk and Materiality in Conducting an Audit,* as amended (AICPA, *Professional*

---

[4] For issuers, certain paragraphs of SAS No. 47, *Audit Risk and Materiality in Conducting an Audit* (AU sec. 312), and SAS No. 99, *Consideration of Fraud in a Financial Statement Audit* (AU sec. 316) have been amended by PCAOB Release 2004-008. See PCAOB Release 2004-008 or the AICPA publication, *PCAOB Standards and Related Rules,* AU secs. 312 and 316 for further guidance.

*Standards*, vol. 1, AU sec. 312). Guidance on the auditor's consideration of fraud in a financial statement audit is presented in SAS No. 99, *Consideration of Fraud in a Financial Statement Audit* (AICPA, *Professional Standards*, vol. 1, AU sec. 316). SAS No. 54, *Illegal Acts by Clients* (AICPA, *Professional Standards*, vol. 1, AU sec. 317), defines the term *illegal acts* and provides guidance on the auditor's consideration of illegal acts in a financial statement audit. Because SAS No. 47, No. 99, and No. 54 are applicable only to audits of financial statements, they are not applicable to a service auditor's engagement. However, in the course of performing procedures at a service organization, a service auditor may become aware of uncorrected errors, fraud, or illegal acts attributable to the service organization's systems, management, or employees, that may affect one or more user organizations. For example, a bank trust department may inadvertently understate the amount of investment income that should be allocated to an employee benefit plan. SAS No. 70, as amended (AU sec. 324.23), states that in such circumstances, unless clearly inconsequential, the service auditor should determine from the appropriate level of the service organization's management whether this information has been communicated to the affected user organizations. If management of the service organization has not communicated this information and is unwilling to do so, the service auditor should inform the service organization's audit committee or others with equivalent authority. If the audit committee does not respond appropriately, the service auditor should consider whether to resign from the engagement. The service auditor generally is not required to confirm with the user organizations that the service organization has communicated such information. If the user organizations have been notified in writing, the service auditor should consider requesting a copy of the written communication. In all cases, judgment should be used in determining what evidence should be obtained concerning the communication of such information and in determining whether the errors are significant enough to require disclosure in the service auditor's report. Unless significant, errors of a routine nature that recently have been identified in a reconciliation, and that are being corrected, generally would not be considered items that should be communicated to affected user organizations.

## Representation Letter From the Service Organization's Management

**4.114** In all engagements, a service auditor should obtain written representations from the service organization's management. The representation letter should be signed by members of the service organization's management who the service auditor believes are responsible for and knowledgeable, directly or through others in the service organization, about the matters covered in the representations. SAS No. 70, as amended (AU sec. 324.61), provides guidance as to the types of representations the service auditor should obtain. Additional matters to be included in the letter will be determined by the circumstances. The refusal by a service organization's management to provide the written representations considered necessary by the service auditor constitutes a limitation on the scope of the engagement that should be considered in forming the service auditor's opinion. The representation letter and the service auditor's report each should be dated as of the completion of fieldwork. An illustrative representation letter for a service auditor's engagement is presented in Appendix B of this Guide.

## Elements of the Service Organization's Description That Are Not Covered by the Service Auditor's Report

**4.115** The service organization's description may contain information that is not covered by the service auditor's report. Examples of such information include the following:

- Information that is not included in the scope of the engagement
- Qualitative information, such as marketing claims, that may not be objectively measurable
- Information that would not be considered relevant to user organizations' internal control as it relates to an audit of financial statements

**4.116** If the service organization wishes to present such information, it should be placed in a separate section of the report entitled "Other Information Provided by the Service Organization," as described in Chapter 3.

**4.117** The fourth standard of reporting of the 10 generally accepted auditing standards in SAS No. 95, *Generally Accepted Auditing Standards* (AICPA, *Professional Standards*, vol. 1, AU sec. 150.02), states, in part:

> In all cases where an auditor's name is associated with financial statements, the report should contain a clear-cut indication of the character of the auditor's work, if any, and the degree of responsibility the auditor is taking.

**4.118** To adhere to the intent of the fourth standard of reporting, the service auditor should disclaim an opinion on information that is not covered by the service auditor's report. For example, this concept can be applied in a situation in which a data processing service organization provides payroll and inventory applications to its customers and the service auditor has been engaged to report only on the payroll application. If the service organization includes information about the inventory application in a separate section of the description, the service auditor should indicate in his or her report that the information about the inventory application is not covered by the service auditor's report. The service auditor's report should clearly identify the services or processing covered by the service auditor's report. The following is a sample explanatory paragraph that should be added to the service auditor's report if information that is not covered by the report is included in the service organization's description:

> The information in section 4 describing Example Computer Service Organization's inventory application is presented by Example Computer Service Organization to provide additional information and is not a part of Example Computer Service Organization's description of controls that may be relevant to user organizations' internal control as it relates to an audit of financial statements. Such information has not been subjected to the procedures applied in the examination of the description of the payroll application, and accordingly, we express no opinion on it.

## Going-Concern Matters

**4.119** In a financial statement audit, the auditor is required to consider whether he or she has identified conditions or events that may indicate there is substantial doubt about an entity's ability to continue as a going concern based on procedures performed and information obtained during the audit. Because of its nature and purpose, a service auditor's engagement does not provide the service auditor with a basis for determining whether there is substantial doubt about an entity's ability to continue as a going concern. Accordingly, a service auditor is not responsible for identifying or reporting going-concern matters related to the service organization when performing a service auditor's engagement.

## Reportable Conditions[5]

**4.120**   The term *reportable conditions* specifically relates to audits of financial statements and not to service auditors' engagements. SAS No. 60, *Communication of Internal Control Related Matters Noted in an Audit* (AICPA, *Professional Standards*, vol. 1, AU sec. 325.02), defines reportable conditions as matters coming to the auditor's attention during a financial statement audit that, in the auditor's judgment, should be communicated to the audit committee, or to individuals with a level of authority and responsibility equivalent to that of an audit committee. These matters are communicated because they represent significant deficiencies in the design or operation of the organization's internal control that could adversely affect the organization's ability to record, process, summarize, and report financial data consistent with management's assertions. A service auditor is not in a position to identify reportable conditions at a service organization and is not responsible for identifying such conditions because a service auditor (1) is not performing an audit of the service organization's financial statements and (2) is not aware of conditions existing at user organizations.

**4.121**   Although a service auditor is not responsible for identifying reportable conditions, SAS No. 70, as amended (AU sec. 324.32 and .47), requires a service auditor to consider conditions that come to his or her attention that preclude the service auditor from obtaining reasonable assurance that specified control objectives would be achieved. The service auditor is required to disclose exceptions in the design or operation of controls that cause the nonachievement of specified control objectives. The service auditor also is required to disclose any other information, irrespective of specified control objectives, that comes to his or her attention that causes him or her to conclude (1) that design deficiencies exist that could adversely affect the ability to record, process, summarize, or report financial data to user organizations without error, and (2) that user organizations would not generally be expected to have controls in place to mitigate such design deficiencies. As stated in Chapter 3, "Using Type 1 and Type 2 Reports," it is the user auditor's responsibility to consider this and other information provided by the service organization when determining whether situations noted in the service auditor's report represent reportable conditions for user organizations.

---

[5] For issuers, the term reportable conditions is replaced with the term significant deficiencies. SAS No. 60 has been superseded and its title changed to AU sec. 325, *Communications About Control Deficiencies in An Audit of Financial Statements*. For audits of financial statements only, SAS No. 60 has been superseded by certain paragraphs of PCAOB Release 2004-008. For integrated audits, SAS No. 60 has been superseded by paragraphs 207–214 of PCAOB Auditing Standard No. 2. (See AICPA, *PCAOB Standards and Related Rules*, AU sec. 325.)

# Related Parties

**4.122**  SAS No. 45, *Omnibus Statement on Auditing Standards—1983* (AICPA, *Professional Standards*, vol. 1, AU sec. 334, "Related Parties"), states:

> An audit performed in accordance with generally accepted auditing standards cannot be expected to provide assurance that all related party transactions will be discovered. Nevertheless, during the course of his audit, the auditor should be aware of the possible existence of material related party transactions that could affect the financial statements and of common ownership or management control relationships for which FASB Statement No. 57 [AC section R36] requires disclosure even though there are no transactions.

**4.123**  Because this concept is related to financial statement audits and not assertions about internal control, there is no requirement for the service organization to disclose such information in its description of controls. However, if a service organization is a subsidiary of or related to another entity, and the service organization believes that such information would be relevant to user organizations, it may be disclosed in the service organization's description.

# Using the Work of Internal Auditors[6]

**4.124**  A service organization may have an internal audit department that performs tests of controls as part of its audit plan. The service auditor may determine that it would be effective and efficient to use the results of testing performed by internal auditors in forming its opinion. In using the work of internal auditors, the service auditor should consider the guidance in SAS No. 65, *The Auditor's Consideration of the Internal Audit Function in an Audit of Financial Statements* (AICPA, *Professional Standards*, vol. 1, AU sec. 322). If the service auditor uses work performed by internal auditors, the service auditor should take responsibility for that work, and should neither make reference to the internal auditors in his or her report nor attribute the performance of the tests and the results of tests to them.

# Distribution of Reports

**4.125**  In most cases the service auditor is engaged by the service organization to perform the service auditor's engagement. However, in some cases the service auditor may be engaged by one or more user organizations. A service auditor should distribute his or her report only to the entity that engaged him or her to perform the examination.

# Board of Directors' Minutes

**4.126**  The service auditor is not required to review minutes of meetings of the service organization's board of directors.

---

[6] For issuers, certain paragraphs of SAS No. 65, *The Auditor's Consideration of the Internal Audit Function in an Audit of Financial Statements,* have been amended by PCAOB Release 2004-008. When performing an integrated audit, refer to paragraphs 108–126 of PCAOB Auditing Standard No. 2 for discussion on using the work of others to alter the nature, timing, and extent of the work that otherwise would have been performed to test controls. See PCAOB Release 2004-008 or the AICPA Publication, *PCAOB Standards and Related Rules*, AU sec. 322.

## Legal Letters

**4.127** The service auditor is not required to obtain a legal letter from the service organization's legal counsel.

## Engagements to Report on Only the General Computer Controls of a Service Organization

**4.128** Service organizations may engage an auditor to report only on its controls related to computer processing. In such instances, the service auditor should determine whether such a report would provide information that would be relevant to user organizations. The discussion in the section "Responsibilities of the Service Auditor" at the beginning of this chapter includes a discussion of the fair presentation of the service organization's description of controls. Such engagements generally are appropriate if the service organization provides only the computer hardware and system software, and user organizations provide their own application software (for example, certain types of data processing outsourcing), or if the user auditors are able to obtain sufficient information about application processing and application controls from other sources, but are unable to obtain information about general computer controls from other sources. If a service organization is responsible for developing or changing application software or providing other transaction processing services in addition to providing hardware or system software, a report on general computer controls may not provide user auditors with a sufficient understanding of the service organization's controls relevant to user organizations' internal control. For the description to be fairly presented in these circumstances, it should also describe the application processing and the flow of transactions.

**4.129** Before accepting an engagement to report on the general computer controls of a service organization that provides more than the hardware and system software for running user organizations' application software, the service auditor should consider, through discussion with management and review of standard contracts, how the report will most likely be used by the user organizations (for example, to plan the audit or to satisfy regulatory requirements). The service auditor is not responsible for contacting the user auditors to determine whether this type of report will meet their needs. If the report is likely to be used by user auditors to plan a financial statement audit, and information is not available from other sources, the service auditor should consider the propriety of accepting such an engagement because it generally will not sufficiently cover all the relevant controls at the service organization.

# Chapter 5

# *Service Organizations That Use Other Service Organizations**

**5.01**   This chapter describes how to apply the guidance in this Guide to situations in which a service organization uses another service organization to perform some or all of the processing of the user organizations' transactions.

**5.02**   As mentioned in previous chapters, a user organization may use a service organization that, in turn, uses another service organization (a *subservice organization*). The subservice organization may perform functions or processing that is part of the user organization's information system as it relates to an audit of financial statements. The subservice organization may be a separate entity from the service organization or may be related to the service organization. To plan the audit and assess control risk, a user auditor may need to consider controls at the service organization (as described in Chapter 1, "Audit Considerations for an Entity That Uses a Service Organization"), and also may need to consider controls at the subservice organization. Similarly, a service auditor engaged to examine controls at a service organization and issue a service auditor's report may need to consider functions performed by a subservice organization and the effect of the subservice organization's controls on the service organization.

**5.03**   This chapter provides guidance for situations in which a subservice organization performs functions that could be part of a user organization's information system as it relates to an audit of financial statements. The concepts and guidance in previous chapters provide the basis for the additional guidance in this chapter; accordingly, readers should consider this chapter in the context of the entire Guide.

## Examples of Subservice Organizations and Subservicing Situations

**5.04**   Examples of subservicing can be found in virtually all types of applications and industries. The following paragraphs illustrate typical subservicing situations for a bank's trust department that provides services to employee benefit plans.

**5.05**   As stated in the introduction of this Guide, a bank trust department that provides services to employee benefit plans may be considered a service organization to those plans. The trust department may perform all of the functions involved in transaction processing (in which case this chapter does not

---

\* Refer to the Preface of this Guide for important information about the applicability of the professional standards to audits of issuers and non-issuers (see definitions in the Preface). As applicable this chapter contains dual referencing to both the AICPA and the PCAOB professional standards. For issuers, certain paragraphs of SAS No. 70, *Service Organizations* (AU sec. 324,) have been amended by PCAOB Release 2004-008. See PCAOB Release 2004-008 or the AICPA Publication *PCAOB Standards and Related Rules*, AU sec. 324 for further guidance. See the PCAOB web site at www.pcaobus.org for information about the effective date of PCAOB Auditing Standard No. 2 and related conforming amendments.

apply), or it may use a subservice organization to perform a portion of the transaction processing. Subservice organizations may perform specific aspects of the transaction processing or may perform all of the transaction processing. Examples of the range of services subservice organizations may perform include the following:

- *Limited functions.* A bank trust department may use one or more subservice organizations to determine the current market price of exchange-traded securities owned by employee benefit plans. Some pricing service organizations specialize in a specific type of security. The trust department may engage several pricing service organizations to determine the price of different types of securities. The trust department also may engage more than one pricing service organization to obtain comparative prices for the same securities and thereby have a basis for determining the reasonableness of the pricing. In the situation described above, the functions performed by each subservice organization are limited. Nevertheless, the functions performed by each subservice organization may be part of the user organization's information systems and may affect assertions in the user organization's financial statements.

- *Moderate functions.* A bank trust department may use a data processing service organization to record the transactions and maintain the related accounting records for the employee benefit plans. In such a situation, the trust department may establish controls over the processing performed by the subservice organization, although, more commonly, the trust department relies on the subservice organization's controls to achieve certain applicable control objectives.

- *Extensive functions.* A bank trust department may use a service organization to perform essentially all of the transaction execution, recording, and processing for the employee benefit plans. In such a situation (which is commonly referred to as *private labeling*), the trust department's functions might be limited to establishing and maintaining the account relationship. The trust department relies on the subservice organization to perform essentially all of the functions and controls that affect user organizations' internal control. In this case, the trust department's controls would have a minimal effect on internal control of the user organizations, and the subservice organization's controls would be significant to the user organizations' internal control and to assertions in the user organizations' financial statements.

## The Effect of a Subservice Organization on a User Organization's Internal Control

**5.06** The involvement of a service organization and a subservice organization in the processing of transactions does not diminish the user auditor's responsibility to obtain a sufficient understanding of the entity's internal control to plan the audit. The use of a service organization that uses a subservice organization may require the user auditor to consider the controls at the service organization and at the subservice organization, depending on the functions each performs.

**5.07** Statement on Auditing Standards (SAS) No. 70, *Service Organizations,* as amended (AICPA, *Professional Standards,* vol. 1, AU sec. 324.06–.17), provides guidance to user auditors on considering the effect of a service organization on the internal control of a user organization. Although SAS No. 70, as amended, does not specifically refer to subservice organizations, if a subservice organization is used, the guidance in SAS No. 70, as amended (AU sec. 324.06–.17), should be interpreted to include the subservice organization. Examples of how the user auditor considers the effect of a subservice organization on the internal control of a user organization are the following:

- In situations in which subservice organizations are used, the interaction described in SAS No. 70, as amended (AU sec. 324.06), would involve the user organization, the service organization, and the subservice organization. The degree of this interaction, as well as the nature and materiality of the transactions processed by the service organization and subservice organization, are the most important factors to consider in determining the significance of the subservice organization's controls to the user organization's internal control.

- The factors mentioned in SAS No. 70, as amended (AU sec. 324.06), which a user auditor considers in determining the significance of controls of a service organization to planning the audit of a user organization's financial statements, should also be considered with respect to a subservice organization.

- When applying the guidance in SAS No. 70, as amended (AU sec. 324.07), to situations involving a subservice organization, the user auditor should consider the available information about both the service organization's and the subservice organization's controls, including (1) information in the user organization's possession, such as user manuals, system overviews, technical manuals, and the contract between the user organization and the service organization and (2) reports on the service organization's and subservice organization's controls, such as reports by service auditors (on the service organization, subservice organization, or the service organization and subservice organization together), internal auditors (the user organization's, the service organization's, or the subservice organization's), or regulatory authorities. Because a user organization typically does not have any contractual relationship with the subservice organization, a user organization should obtain available reports and information about the subservice organization from the service organization.

**5.08** After considering the above factors and evaluating the available information, a user auditor may conclude that he or she has the means to obtain a sufficient understanding of a user organization's internal control to plan the audit. If the user auditor concludes that information is not available to obtain a sufficient understanding to plan the audit, he or she may consider contacting the service organization through the user organization or contacting the subservice organization, through the user and service organizations, to obtain specific information or request that a service auditor be engaged to perform procedures that will supply the necessary information. Alternatively, the user auditor may visit the service organization or subservice organization and perform such procedures.

**5.09** SAS No. 70, as amended (AU sec. 324.11–.16), addresses the approach a user auditor should follow in assessing control risk at a user organization. If a subservice organization is used, the user auditor may need to consider activities at both the service organization and the subservice organization in applying the guidance in these paragraphs.

# Responsibilities of Service Organizations, User Auditors, and Service Auditors if Control Objectives Are Established by the Service Organization

**5.10**   The guidance in Chapter 2, "Form and Content of Service Auditors' Reports," is applicable whether or not a subservice organization is used. In addition to this guidance, Appendixes C and D of this Guide and the remainder of this chapter summarize how the responsibilities of service organizations, user auditors, and service auditors are affected when a subservice organization performs functions that could be significant to user organizations. Functions of a subservice organization that could be significant to user organizations generally would be those functions that could contribute to the achievement of the specified control objectives.

**5.11**   A service auditor engaged to issue a report on the controls of a service organization that uses a subservice organization should consider whether the functions and processing performed by the subservice organization could be significant to the user organizations. If the subservice organization's functions are not significant to the user organizations, Appendixes C and D do not apply and there is no need to further consider the subservice organization's functions in the service auditor's engagement. *Significance* in this case should be determined in the same manner that the significance of a service organization to a user organization is determined as described in SAS No. 70, as amended (AU sec. 324.06), and Chapter 1 of this Guide; that is, based on the nature of the services provided by the subservice organization to the service organization and considered in reference to the user organizations.

## Responsibilities of Service Organizations

**5.12**   If the service organization establishes the control objectives, the service organization's description of controls should include the following items:

- A description of the controls at the service organization that may be relevant to user organizations' internal control, as described in SAS No. 70, as amended (AU sec. 324.26), and Chapter 2 of this Guide.
- The control objectives established by the service organization, as described in SAS No. 70, as amended (AU sec. 324.34*a*), and Chapter 2 of this Guide.

These items are required regardless of whether a subservice organization is involved.

**5.13**   As discussed in SAS No. 70, as amended (AU sec. 324.35), the control objectives should be reasonable in the circumstances and consistent with the service organization's contractual obligations, irrespective of whether the service organization uses a subservice organization. If the service organization fails to include control objectives that would be consistent with its contractual obligations to user organizations, the service auditor should discuss the matter with the service organization's management and request that management amend the description by adding the appropriate control objective(s). If the service organization's management does not amend the description to include the recommended control objective(s), the service auditor should add an explanatory paragraph before the opinion paragraph (the first opinion paragraph in a type 2 report) of the service auditor's report identifying the omitted control objective(s). In addition, the first sentence of the opinion paragraph (the first opinion paragraph in a type 2 report) should be modified as indicated in Chapter 4 of this Guide.

**5.14** In addition to describing its controls and control objectives, a service organization that uses a subservice organization should describe the functions and nature of the processing performed by the subservice organization in sufficient detail for user auditors to understand the significance of the subservice organization's functions to the processing of the user organizations' transactions. Ordinarily, disclosure of the identity of the subservice organization is not required. However, if the service organization determines that the identity of the subservice organization would be relevant to user organizations, the name of the subservice organization may be included in the description. The purpose of the description of the functions and nature of the processing performed by the subservice organization is to alert user organizations and their auditors to the fact that another entity (the subservice organization) is involved in the processing of the user organizations' transactions and to summarize the functions the subservice organization performs.

**5.15** The service organization determines whether its description of controls will include the relevant controls of the subservice organization. The two alternative methods of presenting the description are the following:

- *The carve-out method.* The subservice organization's relevant control objectives and controls are excluded from the description and from the scope of the service auditor's engagement. The service organization states in the description that the subservice organization's controls and related control objectives are omitted from the description and that the control objectives in the report include only the objectives the service organization's controls are intended to achieve.

- *The inclusive method.* The subservice organization's relevant controls are included in the description and in the scope of the engagement. The description should clearly differentiate between controls of the service organization and controls of the subservice organization. The set of control objectives includes all of the control objectives a user auditor would expect both the service organization and the subservice organization to achieve. To accomplish this, the service organization should coordinate the preparation and presentation of the description of controls with the subservice organization.

In either method, the service organization includes in its description of controls a description of the functions and nature of the processing performed by the subservice organization.

**5.16** Although the inclusive method provides more information to user auditors, it may not be appropriate or feasible in all circumstances. In determining which approach to follow, the service organization should consider (1) the nature and extent of information about the subservice organization that user auditors will require and (2) the practical difficulties entailed in implementing the inclusive method as described in the following section.[1]

---

[1] This Guide does not provide for the option of having a service auditor make references to or rely on a subservice auditor's report as the basis, in part, for a service auditor's opinion.

## Responsibilities of User Auditors

**5.17**   If the functions performed by the subservice organization are limited, the carve-out method generally will provide user auditors with sufficient information about the subservice organization because the description will indicate the functions performed by the subservice organization and may include information about controls exercised by the service organization over the activities of the subservice organization. If the functions performed by the subservice organization are more extensive, the user auditor may require more information about the subservice organization's controls. Such information may be available from other sources, such as those listed in SAS No. 70, as amended (AU sec. 324.09), which include systems overviews, technical manuals, and reports on the subservice organization's controls, such as reports by a subservice auditor, internal auditors, or a regulatory authority.

**5.18**   An inclusive report generally is most useful in the following circumstances:

- The subservice organization's functions are extensive.
- User auditors require more information than that provided by the carve-out method.
- Information from other sources is not readily available.

**5.19**   However, this approach is difficult to implement and may be impossible to execute in certain circumstances. The approach requires extensive planning and communication between the service auditor, the service organization, and the subservice organization. Both the service organization and the subservice organization must agree on this approach before it is adopted. Matters such as the following must be coordinated by all of the parties involved:

- The scope and timing of the examination
- The responsibilities for the preparation and content of the service organization's and subservice organization's description of controls
- The timing of the tests of controls
- Responsibilities for the content of the representation letters and signatures to be obtained
- Other administrative matters

**5.20**   Such issues become more complex if multiple subservice organizations are involved. The inclusive approach is facilitated if the service organization and the subservice organization are related parties or have a contractual relationship that provides for inclusive reports and visits by service auditors. If the inclusive method is not a practical or feasible alternative and additional information is required, the user auditor should consider the guidance in SAS No. 70, as amended (AU sec. 324.10).

**5.21**   If the service organization establishes the control objectives, the user auditor should determine whether the report meets the user auditor's needs. If the user auditor needs additional information about the functions performed by the subservice organization or about the controls at the subservice organization, the user auditor should consider obtaining such information about the subservice organization in the manner described in SAS No. 70, as amended (AU sec. 324.09–.21).

## Responsibilities of Service Auditors

**5.22**  If the service organization establishes the control objectives, the service auditor should:

- Disclose in the service auditor's report that the control objectives were established by the service organization, as required by SAS No. 70, as amended (AU sec. 324.29c and .44c). (The service auditor should be satisfied that the control objectives are reasonable in the circumstances and consistent with the service organization's contractual obligations, as required by SAS No. 70, as amended (AU sec. 324.35).

- Report on (1) the fairness of the presentation of the description of controls placed in operation, (2) whether the controls were suitably designed to achieve specified control objectives, and (3) for type 2 reports, whether the controls that were tested were operating with sufficient effectiveness to achieve the related control objectives.

These requirements also are applicable if a subservice organization is not involved.

**5.23**  If the functions and processing performed by the subservice organization are significant to the processing of the user organizations' transactions, and the service organization does not disclose the existence of a subservice organization and the functions it performs, the service auditor should request that management of the service organization amend the description to disclose the required information. If management does not amend the description, the service auditor should issue a qualified or adverse opinion as to the fairness of the presentation of the description of controls.

**5.24**  If the service organization has adopted the carve-out method, the service auditor should modify the scope paragraph of the service auditor's report to briefly summarize the functions and nature of the processing performed by the subservice organization. This summary ordinarily would be briefer than the information provided by the service organization in its description of the functions and nature of the processing performed by the subservice organization. The service auditor should include a statement in the scope paragraph of the service auditor's report indicating that the description of controls includes only the controls and related control objectives of the service organization; therefore, the service auditor's examination does not extend to controls of the subservice organization. An example of the scope paragraph of a service auditor's report using the carve-out method is presented in the following section. Additional or modified report language is shown in boldface italics.

**5.25**  Although under the carve-out method, the control objectives typically address only controls at the service organization, situations may arise in which the service organization specifies control objectives whose achievement depends on controls at a subservice organization. In these situations, the service auditor should consider modifying the scope and opinion paragraphs of the report in a manner similar to the modifications made for user control considerations, as specified in SAS No. 70, as amended (AU sec. 324.54, footnote 4).

**5.26**  When subservice organizations are used, the service auditor should consider the completeness of the service organization's control objectives. For example, a service organization may adopt the carve-out method for a computer processing subservice organization that it uses, but still maintain responsibility for restricting logical access to the system to properly authorized individuals.

In this situation, the service organization should have a control objective that addresses restricting logical access to the system.

**5.27**  Also, the service auditor should consider whether the description of the service organization's control objectives portrays the control objectives the controls are designed to achieve. For example, a fund accounting agent should not have a control objective stating that "Controls provide reasonable assurance that portfolio securities are properly valued" because the fund accounting agent does not have responsibility for the validity or propriety of the vendor or broker-supplied market values. Instead, the control objective may state, "Controls provide reasonable assurance that portfolio securities are valued using current prices obtained from sources authorized by the customer," to more accurately reflect what the controls are designed to achieve.

## Sample Service Auditor's Report Using the Carve-Out Method

**5.28**  An example of a service auditor's report using the carve out method is presented below. Additional or modified report language is shown in boldface italics.

Independent Service Auditor's Report

To the Board of Directors of Example Trust Organization:

We have examined the accompanying description of the controls of Example Trust Organization applicable to the processing of transactions for users of the institutional trust division. Our examination included procedures to obtain reasonable assurance about whether (1) the accompanying description presents fairly, in all material respects, the aspects of Example Trust Organization's controls that may be relevant to a user organization's internal control as it relates to an audit of financial statements; (2) the controls included in the description were suitably designed to achieve the control objectives specified in the description, if those controls were complied with satisfactorily, and user organizations[2] applied the controls contemplated in the design of Example Trust Organization's controls; and (3) such controls had been placed in operation as of June 30, 20XX. *Example Trust Organization uses a computer processing service organization for all of its computerized application processing. The accompanying description includes only those controls and related control objectives of Example Trust Organization, and does not include controls and related control objectives of the computer processing service organization. Our examination did not extend to controls of the computer processing service organization.* The control objectives were specified by the management of Example

---

[2] If the application of controls by a subservice organization is necessary to achieve the specified control objectives, the service auditor's report may be modified to include the phrase "and subservice organizations applied the controls contemplated in the design of Example Trust Organization's controls," in both the scope and opinion paragraphs. The sample report presented above also includes a reference to the application of controls by user organizations. When reference is made to both user organization controls and subservice organization controls, a phrase such as the following could be inserted, "and user organizations and subservice organizations applied the controls contemplated in the design of Example Trust Organization's controls."

Trust Organization. Our examination was performed in accordance with standards established by the American Institute of Certified Public Accountants and included those procedures we considered necessary in the circumstances to obtain a reasonable basis for rendering our opinion.

In our opinion, the accompanying description of the aforementioned controls presents fairly, in all material respects, the relevant aspects of Example Trust Organization's controls that had been placed in operation as of June 30, 20XX. Also, in our opinion, the controls, as described, are suitably designed to provide reasonable assurance that the specified control objectives would be achieved if the described controls were complied with satisfactorily[2] and user organizations applied the controls contemplated in the design of Example Trust Organization's controls.

In addition to the procedures we considered necessary to render our opinion as expressed in the previous paragraph, we applied tests to specific controls, listed in section 3, to obtain evidence about their effectiveness in meeting the control objectives, described in section 3, during the period from January 1, 20XX, to June 30, 20XX. The specific controls and the nature, timing, extent, and results of the tests are listed in section 3. This information has been provided to user organizations of Example Trust Organization and to their auditors to be taken into consideration, along with information about the internal control of user organizations, when making assessments of control risk for user organizations. In our opinion, the controls that were tested, as described in section 3, were operating with sufficient effectiveness to provide reasonable, but not absolute, assurance that the control objectives specified in section 3 were achieved during the period from January 1, 20XX, to June 30, 20XX.

The relative effectiveness and significance of specific controls at Example Trust Organization and their effect on assessments of control risk at user organizations are dependent on their interaction with the controls, and other factors present at individual user organizations. We have performed no procedures to evaluate the effectiveness of controls at individual user organizations.

The description of controls at Example Trust Organization is as of June 30, 20XX, and the information about tests of the operating effectiveness of specific controls covers the period from January 1, 20XX, to June 30, 20XX. Any projection of such information to the future is subject to the risk that, because of change, the description may no longer portray the controls in existence. The potential effectiveness of specific controls at the Example Trust Organization is subject to inherent limitations and, accordingly, errors or fraud may occur and not be detected. Furthermore, the projection of any

---

[2] See footnote 2, para 5.28.

conclusions, based on our findings, to future periods is subject
to the risk that (1) changes made to the system or controls,
(2) changes in processing requirements, or (3) changes required because of the passage of time may alter the validity
of such conclusions.[3]

This report is intended solely for use by the management of
Example Trust Organization, users of its institutional trust
division, and the independent auditors of its users.

July 10, 20XX

**5.29** If the service organization has used the inclusive method, the service auditor should perform procedures comparable to those described in SAS
No. 70, as amended (AU sec. 324.12). Such procedures may include performing
tests of the service organization's controls over the activities of the subservice
organization or performing procedures at the subservice organization. If the
service auditor will be performing procedures at the subservice organization,
the service organization should arrange for such procedures. The service auditor should recognize that the subservice organization generally is not the client
for the engagement. Accordingly, in these circumstances, the service auditor
should determine whether it will be possible to obtain the required evidence
to support the portion of the opinion covering the subservice organization and
whether it will be possible to obtain an appropriate letter of representations
regarding the subservice organization's controls.

## Sample Service Auditor's Report Using the Inclusive Method

**5.30** An example of a service auditor's report using the inclusive method
is presented below. Additional or modified report language is shown in boldface
italics.

Independent Service Auditor's Report

To the Board of Directors of Example Trust Organization:

We have examined the accompanying description of the controls of Example Trust Organization **and Computer Processing Service Organization, an independent service
organization that provides computer processing services to Example Trust Organization,** applicable to the
processing of transactions for users of the institutional trust
division. Our examination included procedures to obtain reasonable assurance about whether (1) the accompanying description presents fairly, in all material respects, the aspects
of Example Trust Organization's and **Computer Processing
Service Organization's** controls that may be relevant to a
user organization's internal control as it relates to an audit
of financial statements; (2) the controls included in the description were suitably designed to achieve the control objectives specified in the description, if those controls were

---

[3] This sentence has been expanded to describe the risks of projecting any evaluation of the
controls to future periods because of the failure to make needed changes to a system or controls,
as provided for in Interpretation No. 5, "Statements About the Risk of Projecting Evaluations of
the Effectiveness of Controls to Future Periods," of SAS No. 70, *Service Organizations*, as amended
(AICPA, *Professional Standards*, vol. 1, AU sec. 9324.38–.40).

complied with satisfactorily,[4] and user organizations applied the controls contemplated in the design of Example Trust Organization's controls; and (3) such controls had been placed in operation as of June 30, 20XX. The control objectives were specified by the management of Example Trust Organization. Our examination was performed in accordance with standards established by the American Institute of Certified Public Accountants and included those procedures we considered necessary in the circumstances to obtain a reasonable basis for rendering our opinion.

In our opinion, the accompanying description of the aforementioned controls presents fairly, in all material respects, the relevant aspects of Example Trust Organization's *and Computer Processing Service Organization's* controls that had been placed in operation as of June 30, 20XX. Also, in our opinion, the controls, as described, are suitably designed to provide reasonable assurance that the specified control objectives would be achieved if the described controls were complied with satisfactorily[4] and user organizations applied the controls contemplated in the design of Example Trust Organization's controls.

In addition to the procedures we considered necessary to render our opinion as expressed in the previous paragraph, we applied tests to specific controls, listed in section 3, to obtain evidence about their effectiveness in meeting the control objectives, described in section 3, during the period from January 1, 20XX, to June 30, 20XX. The specific controls and the nature, timing, extent, and results of the tests are listed in section 3. This information has been provided to user organizations of Example Trust Organization and to their auditors to be taken into consideration, along with information about the internal control of user organizations, when making assessments of control risk for user organizations.

In our opinion, the controls that were tested, as described in section 3, were operating with sufficient effectiveness to provide reasonable, but not absolute, assurance that the control objectives specified in section 3 were achieved during the period from January 1, 20XX, to June 30, 20XX.

The relative effectiveness and significance of specific controls at Example Trust Organization *and Computer Processing Service Organization* and their effect on assessments of control risk at user organizations are dependent on their interaction with the controls and other factors present

---

[4] If the application of controls by a subservice organization that is not covered by the report is necessary to achieve the specified control objectives, the service auditor's report may be modified to include the phrase "and subservice organizations applied the controls contemplated in the design of Example Trust Organization's controls," in both the scope and opinion paragraphs. The sample report presented above also includes a reference to the application of controls by user organizations. When reference is made to both user organization controls and subservice organization controls, a phrase such as the following could be inserted, "and user organizations and subservice organizations applied the controls contemplated in the design of Example Trust Organization's controls."

at individual user organizations. We have performed no procedures to evaluate the effectiveness of controls at individual
user organizations.

The description of controls at Example Trust Organization
and *Computer Processing Service Organization* is as of
June 30, 20XX, and the information about tests of the operating effectiveness of specific controls covers the period from
January 1, 20XX, to June 30, 20XX. Any projection of such
information to the future is subject to the risk that, because
of change, the description may no longer portray the controls
in existence. The potential effectiveness of specific controls at
the Example Trust Organization *and Computer Processing Service Organization* is subject to inherent limitations
and, accordingly, errors or fraud may occur and not be detected. Furthermore, the projection of any conclusions, based
on our findings, to future periods is subject to the risk that
(1) changes made to the system or controls, (2) changes in
processing requirements, or (3) changes required because of
the passage of time may alter the validity of such conclusions.[5]

This report is intended solely for use by the management of
Example Trust Organization, users of its institutional trust
division, and the independent auditors of its users.

July 10, 20XX

**5.31**  Performing procedures at the subservice organization will require
coordination and communication between the service organization, the subservice organization, and the service auditor. This alternative may be less difficult
to implement if the service organization and the subservice organization are
related or if the contract between the service organization and the subservice
organization provides for visits by the service organization's auditors.

**5.32**  A service auditor should question accepting an engagement in which
a service organization functions primarily as an intermediary between the user
organizations and the subservice organization, and performs few or no functions
that affect transaction processing for user organizations. If a service organization's controls do not contribute to the achievement of any control objectives, a
report on its controls would not be useful to user auditors in planning the audit.

## Responsibilities of Service Organizations, User Auditors, and the Service Auditors if Control Objectives Are Established by an Outside Party

**5.33**  If an outside party establishes the control objectives, the responsibilities of the service organization, user auditors, and service auditors do not
change except for the following items, as indicated in the table in Appendix D.

- The service organization should describe the control objectives established by the outside party and the source of the control objectives.

---

[5] This sentence has been expanded to describe the risks of projecting any evaluation of the
controls to future periods because of failure to make needed changes to a system or controls, as
provided for in Auditing Interpretation No. 5, "Statements About the Risk of Projecting Evaluations
of the Effectiveness of Controls to the Future," of SAS No. 70, as amended (AU sec. 9324.38–.40).

- The service auditor does not need to determine whether the control objectives are reasonable in the circumstances and consistent with the service organization's contractual obligations because the control objectives have been established by an outside party.

## Subservice Organizations That Hold and Service Securities

**5.34** Many service organizations, such as bank trust departments, use subservice organizations to *hold* and *service* securities. SAS No. 92, *Auditing Derivative Instruments, Hedging Activities, and Investments in Securities* (AICPA, *Professional Standards,* vol. 1, AU sec. 332),[6] defines *holding* securities as maintaining custody of securities that are either in physical or electronic form. It defines *servicing* securities as performing ancillary services such as:

- Collecting dividend and interest income and distributing that income to the entity.
- Receiving notification of corporate actions.
- Receiving notification of security purchase and sale transactions.
- Receiving payments from purchasers and disbursing proceeds to sellers for security purchase and sale transactions.
- Maintaining records of securities transactions for the entity.

**5.35** In such situations, confirmation procedures may provide substantive audit evidence of the existence of securities and ownership by the user organizations. A service auditor's report on the custody and safekeeping subservice organization may also provide useful information to user organizations, user auditors, service organizations, and service auditors regarding the controls over custody, safekeeping, and any other functions such custodians may perform.

---

[6] For issuers, PCAOB Release 2004-008 amends paragraph 11 of SAS No. 92 by adding that when performing an integrated audit, PCAOB Auditing Standard No. 2 states, "the auditor must obtain sufficient competent evidence about the design and operating effectiveness of controls over all relevant financial statement assertions related to all significant accounts and disclosures in the financial statements." Therefore, in an integrated audit, if a company's investment in derivatives and securities represents a significant account, the auditor's understanding of controls should include controls over derivatives and securities transactions from their initiation to their inclusion in the financial statements and should encompass controls placed in operation by the entity and service organizations whose services are part of the entity's information system.

**AAG-SRV 5.35**

# Appendix A

# Examples of Service Auditors' Reports, Descriptions of Controls Placed in Operation, and Descriptions of Tests of Operating Effectiveness

**A.1** Although Statement on Auditing Standards (SAS) No. 70, *Service Organizations*, as amended (AICPA, *Professional Standards,* vol. 1, AU sec. 324), is fairly specific about the information that should be included in a type 1 or type 2 report, it is not specific about the format for these reports. Service organizations and service auditors may organize and present the required information in a variety of formats. This appendix contains two examples of type 2 reports. The concepts concerning the form and content of these illustrative type 2 reports also apply to type 1 reports, which are not illustrated in this appendix. The reports are for Example Computer Service Organization and Example Trust Organization and illustrate the reporting guidance presented in Chapter 2, "Form and Content of Service Auditors' Reports"; Chapter 3, "Using Type 1 and Type 2 Reports"; and Chapter 4, "Performing a Service Auditor's Engagement." The examples illustrate two different methods of organizing a type 2 report. For brevity, the illustrative reports do not include everything that might be described in a type 2 report. Ellipses (...) or notes to readers indicate places where detail has been omitted from the illustrative reports.

**A.2** The control objectives and controls specified by the service organizations in the illustrative reports, as well as the tests performed by the service auditors, are presented for illustrative purposes only. They are not intended to represent a complete or standard set of control objectives, controls, or tests of operating effectiveness that would be appropriate for all service organizations. The determination of the appropriate control objectives, controls, and tests of operating effectiveness for a specific service organization can be made only in the context of specific facts and circumstances. Accordingly, it is expected that actual service auditors' reports will contain differing control objectives, controls, and tests of operating effectiveness.

**A.3** The illustrative type 2 report in Example 1 for Example Computer Service Organization contains the four sections described in Chapter 2 of this Guide; however, the control objectives and related controls are omitted from section 2, "Example Computer Service Organization's Description of Controls," and are presented only in section 3, "Information Provided by the Service Auditor." The purpose of this format is to eliminate the redundancy that would result if the control objectives and related controls were listed in sections 2 and 3 of the report. A paragraph is included in section 2 of the report alerting readers to the fact that the control objectives and related controls presented in section 3 are the responsibility of the service organization and should be considered part of the service organization's description. In this example, the reader is to assume that all of the control objectives were tested for operating effectiveness.

**A.4** The second illustrative type 2 report, Example 2, is based on Example Trust Organization. In this type 2 report, the service organization's control objectives and related controls, the tests of operating effectiveness performed by the service auditor, and the results of the tests are presented in section 2, "Example Trust Organization's Description of Controls." As in Example 1, the objective of this method of presentation is to avoid the redundancy that would result from presenting the same material in two sections. A paragraph is included in section 3 indicating that the tests of operating effectiveness and results of the tests presented in section 2 are the responsibility of the service auditor and should be considered part of the service auditor's section. As in Example 1, the reader is to assume that all of the control objectives were tested for operating effectiveness.

## Example 1

**Example Computer Service Organization**

**Report on Controls Placed in Operation
and Tests of Operating Effectiveness**

**Table of Contents**

---

\* Items marked with an asterisk are presented in the table of contents for illustrative purposes only and are either included in part in or left entirely out of this illustrative type 2 report.

**3.** Information Provided by the Service Auditor

Control Objectives, Related Controls, and Tests of Operating Effectiveness

    General Computer Controls

        Systems Development and Maintenance

        Access

        Computer Operations

    Savings Application Controls

    Mortgage Loan Application Controls*

    Consumer Loan Application Controls*

**4.** Other Information Provided by Example Computer Service Organization

Description of Other Applications*

    Commercial Loan*

    General Ledger*

Description of Planned Changes to Applications*

1

**Independent Service Auditor's Report**

To the Board of Directors of Example Computer Service Organization:

We have examined the accompanying description of controls related to the Savings, Mortgage Loan, and Consumer Loan applications of Example Computer Service Organization. Our examination included procedures to obtain reasonable assurance about whether (1) the accompanying description presents fairly, in all material respects, the aspects of Example Computer Service Organization's controls that may be relevant to a user organization's internal control as it relates to an audit of financial statements; (2) the controls included in the description were suitably designed to achieve the control objectives specified in the description, if those controls were complied with satisfactorily and user organizations applied the controls contemplated in the design of Example Computer Service Organization's controls; and (3) such controls had been placed in operation as of June 30, 20XX. The control objectives were specified by the management of Example Computer Service Organization. Our examination was performed in accordance with standards established by the American Institute of Certified Public Accountants and included those procedures we considered necessary in the circumstances to obtain a reasonable basis for rendering our opinion.

In our opinion, the accompanying description of the aforementioned applications presents fairly, in all material respects, the relevant aspects of Example Computer Service Organization's controls that had been placed in operation as of June 30, 20XX. Also, in our opinion, the controls, as described, are suitably designed to provide reasonable assurance that the specified control objectives would be achieved if the described controls were complied with satisfactorily and user organizations applied the controls contemplated in the design of Example Computer Service Organization's controls.

---

  * See footnote * in page 74.

In addition to the procedures we considered necessary to render our opinion as expressed in the previous paragraph, we applied tests to specific controls, which are presented in section 3 of this report, to obtain evidence about their effectiveness in meeting the related control objectives described in section 3, during the period from January 1, 20XX, to June 30, 20XX. The specific controls and the nature, timing, extent, and results of the tests are listed in section 3. This information has been provided to user organizations of Example Computer Service Organization and to their auditors to be taken into consideration, along with information about the internal control at user organizations, when making assessments of control risk for user organizations. In our opinion the controls that were tested, as described in section 3, were operating with sufficient effectiveness to provide reasonable, but not absolute, assurance that the control objectives specified in section 3 were achieved during the period from January 1, 20XX, to June 30, 20XX.

The relative effectiveness and significance of specific controls at Example Computer Service Organization and their effect on assessments of control risk at user organizations are dependent on their interaction with the controls and other factors present at individual user organizations. We have performed no procedures to evaluate the effectiveness of controls at individual user organizations.

The description of controls at Example Computer Service Organization is as of June 30, 20XX, and information about tests of the operating effectiveness of specific controls covers the period from January 1, 20XX, to June 30, 20XX. Any projection of such information to the future is subject to the risk that, because of change, the description may no longer portray the controls in existence. The potential effectiveness of specific controls at the Service Organization is subject to inherent limitations and, accordingly, errors or fraud may occur and not be detected. Furthermore, the projection of any conclusions, based on our findings, to future periods is subject to the risk that (1) changes made to the system or controls, (2) changes in processing requirements, or (3) changes required because of the passage of time may alter the validity of such conclusions.[1]

The information included in section 4 of this report is presented by Example Computer Service Organization to provide additional information to user organizations and is not a part of Example Computer Service Organization's description of controls placed in operation. The information in section 4 has not been subjected to the procedures applied in the examination of the description of the controls related to the Savings, Mortgage Loan, and Consumer Loan applications, and accordingly, we express no opinion on it.

This report is intended solely for use by the management of Example Computer Service Organization, its users, and the independent auditors of its users.[2]

July 10, 20XX

---

[1] This sentence has been expanded to describe the risks of projecting any evaluation of the controls to future periods because of the failure to make needed changes to a system or controls, as provided for in Auditing Interpretation No. 5, "Statements About the Risk of Projecting Evaluations of the Effectiveness of Controls to Future Periods,"of Statement on Auditing Standards (SAS) No. 70, *Service Organizations*, as amended (AICPA, *Professional Standards*, vol. 1, AU sec. 9324.38–.40).

[2] SAS No. 87, *Restricting the Use of an Auditor's Report* (AICPA, *Professional Standards*, vol. 1, AU sec. 532.19c), presents the following illustrative restricted-use paragraph:

> This report is intended solely for the information and use of [*the specified parties*] and is not intended to be and should not be used by anyone other than these specified parties.

The language in that paragraph may be used in a service auditor's report.

2

### Example Computer Service Organization's Description of Controls

## Overview of Operations

Example Computer Service Organization (the Organization) is located in Los Angeles, California, and provides computer services primarily to user organizations in the financial services industry. Applications enable user organizations to process savings, mortgage loan, consumer loan, commercial loan, and general ledger transactions. This description addresses only controls related to the Savings, Mortgage Loan, and Consumer Loan applications. Section 4 of this report contains certain information about the Commercial Loan and General Ledger applications.

Numerous terminals located at user organizations are connected to the Organization through leased lines that provide online, real-time access to the applications. The Organization processes transactions using one ABC central processor under the control of Operating System Release 2.1....

## Relevant Aspects of the Control Environment, Risk Assessment, and Monitoring

### Control Environment

Operations are under the direction of the president and the board of directors of the Organization. The board of directors has established an audit committee that oversees the internal audit function. The Organization employs a staff of approximately 35 people and is supported by the functional areas listed here.

- *Administration and systems development.* Coordinates all aspects of the service organization's operations, including service billing. Identifies areas requiring controls and implements those controls. Performs systems planning, development, and implementation. Reviews network operations and telecommunications and performs disaster-recovery planning and database administration.

- *Customer support.* Supports end users in all aspects of their use of the application system including research and resolution of identified problems. Administers application security (including passwords), changes to application parameters, and the distribution of user documentation.

- *Application programming.* Performs regular maintenance programming, programming for user-requested enhancements, and updates the systems documentation.

- *Terminal support.* Performs end-user terminal training. Researches and resolves terminal and network problems and performs timely installations of enhancements to terminal and network software.

- *Operations.* Manages daily computer operations, nightly production processing, report production and distribution, and system utilization and capacities.

- *Marketing.* Provides analysis for new business prospects and new product planning.

**AAG-SRV APP A**

The managers of each of the functional areas report to the director of information systems.

The Organization's employees are not authorized to initiate or authorize transactions, to change or modify user files except through normal production procedures, or to correct user errors. All shifts at the Organization are managed by shift supervisors and the director of information systems. Incident reports, processing logs, job schedules, and equipment activity reports are monitored by the director of information systems. These reports track daily processing activities and identify hardware and software problems and system usage.

Weekly management meetings are held to discuss special processing requests, operational performance, and the development and maintenance of projects in process.

Written position descriptions for employees are maintained by the director of information systems and the personnel department. The descriptions are reviewed annually and revised as necessary.

References are sought and background, credit, and security checks are conducted for all Organization personnel hired. The confidentiality of user-organization information is stressed during the new-employee orientation program and is emphasized in the personnel manual issued to each employee. The Organization provides a mandatory orientation program to all full-time employees and encourages employees to attend other formal outside training. An internal supervisory training program was recently initiated.

Employees are required to take vacation in accordance with the Organization's policy, which requires that all employees who are eligible for two or more weeks of vacation take off five consecutive business days during each calendar year. No employee may take vacation during the last week or first ten days of each quarter. Vacation must be taken in the calendar year in which it is earned.

The Organization's policy requires that after three months of employment, new employees receive a written performance evaluation from their supervisors, and that all employees receive an annual written performance evaluation and salary review. These reviews are based on employee-stated goals and objectives that are prepared and reviewed with the employee's supervisor. Completed appraisals are reviewed by senior management and become a permanent part of the employee's personnel file.

The internal auditors provide the audit committee with an assessment of controls. The internal auditors execute an information-technology internal audit program, and follow up on any operational exceptions or concerns that may arise. The internal auditors use audit software to perform various recalculations and analyses using actual production data in an off-line mode.

## Risk Assessment

The Organization has placed into operation a risk assessment process to identify and manage risks that could affect the Organization's ability to provide reliable transaction processing for user organizations. This process requires management to identify significant risks in their areas of responsibility and to implement appropriate measures to address those risks. The agenda for each quarterly management meeting includes a discussion of these matters. This process has identified risks resulting from the nature of the services the Organization provides, and management has implemented various measures to manage those risks.

## Monitoring

The Organization's management and supervisory personnel monitor the quality of internal control performance as a routine part of their activities. To assist them in this monitoring, the Organization has implemented a series of "key indicator" management reports that measure the results of various processes involved in processing transactions for user organizations. Key indicator reports include reports of actual transaction processing volumes compared with anticipated volumes, actual processing times compared with scheduled times, and actual system availability and response times compared with established service level goals and standards. All exceptions to normal or scheduled processing related to hardware, software, or procedural problems are logged, reported, and resolved daily. Key indicator reports are reviewed daily and weekly by appropriate levels of management, and action is taken as necessary.

# Information and Communication

## Information Systems

The Organization's Savings, Mortgage Loan, and Consumer Loan applications are part of an integrated software system. This system provides online, real-time processing of monetary and nonmonetary transactions and provides batch and memo postprocessing capabilities. Processing activities are divided into online and off-line processing segments. During ordinary business hours, user organizations may make inquiries and enter monetary and nonmonetary transactions through various terminals, including teller terminals. Additional transactions are transmitted from automatic teller machines (ATMs), the Federal Reserve Bank, and user banks. Such transactions are received via electronic data transmission or via tape delivered by courier.

Each application uses the standard operating system and related systems software to interact with terminals, to accept data, to apply prescribed processes to data, to maintain an audit trail, and to respond to inquiries.

Online daily processing occurs during preestablished hours when user organizations are open. Monetary, nonmonetary, and inquiry transactions are entered at teller terminals located at branch offices of user organizations serviced by the Organization. Nonmonetary and inquiry transactions are entered at other terminals designated as administrative terminals in branch offices and other offices of user organizations. Terminals are linked to the online data communications network through leased telephone lines. Telecommunications software polls the terminals in the network for available input transactions....

Off-line daily processing is performed in accordance with daily schedules and generally occurs when the online system is not running. These programs determine whether control totals agree with the totals of related detail accounts, and produce daily and special-request reports.

Following is a description of the Savings, Mortgage Loan, and Consumer Loan applications.

**AAG-SRV APP A**

## Savings Application

The Savings application maintains account balances based on deposits, withdrawals, earnings postings, journal debits and credits, and other transactions. The application provides for online data entry and inquiry functions and online, real-time posting of monetary and nonmonetary transactions entered through teller terminals....

> **Note to Readers:** The remainder of the description of the Savings application and the descriptions of the Mortgage Loan and Consumer Loan applications are not presented in this sample type 2 report.

## Communication

The Organization has implemented various methods of communication to ensure that all employees understand their individual roles and responsibilities over transaction processing and controls, and to ensure that significant events are communicated in a timely manner. These methods include orientation and training programs for newly hired employees, a monthly Organization newsletter that summarizes significant events and changes occurring during the month and planned for the following month, and the use of electronic mail messages to communicate time-sensitive messages and information. Managers also hold periodic staff meetings as appropriate. Every employee has a written position description, and every position description includes the responsibility to communicate significant issues and exceptions to an appropriate higher level of authority within the organization in a timely manner.

The Organization also has implemented various methods of communication to ensure that user organizations understand the role and responsibilities of the Organization in processing their transactions, and to ensure that significant events are communicated to users in a timely manner. These methods include the Organization's active participation in quarterly user group meetings, the monthly Organization newsletter, which summarizes the significant events and changes during the month and planned for the following month, and the user liaison who maintains contact with designated user representatives to inform them of new issues and developments. Users also are encouraged to communicate questions and problems to their liaison, and such matters are logged and tracked until resolved, with the resolution also reported to the user organization.

Personnel in Example Computer Service Organization's customer support unit provide ongoing communication with customers. The customer support unit maintains records of problems reported by customers and problems or incidents noted during processing, and monitors such items until they are resolved. The customer support unit also communicates information regarding changes in processing schedules, system enhancements, and other information to customers.

## Control Objectives and Related Controls

The Organization's control objectives and related controls are included in section 3 of this report, "Information Provided by the Service Auditor," to eliminate the redundancy that would result from listing them in this section and repeating them in section 3. Although the control objectives and related controls are included in section 3, they are, nevertheless, an integral part of the Organization's description of controls.

> **Note to Readers**: The paragraph above has been included to clearly indicate to readers that the control objectives and related controls are an integral part of the Organization's description even though they have been presented in the service auditor's section to reduce redundancy in the report.

## User Control Considerations

The Organization's applications were designed with the assumption that certain controls would be implemented by user organizations. In certain situations, the application of specific controls at user organizations is necessary to achieve certain control objectives included in this report. In such instances, the required user-organization controls are identified under the related control objective in section 3 of this report.

This section describes additional controls that should be in operation at user organizations to complement the controls at the Organization. User auditors should consider whether the following controls have been placed in operation at user organizations:

- Controls to provide reasonable assurance that changes to processing options (parameters) are appropriately authorized, approved, and implemented
- Controls to provide reasonable assurance that transactions are appropriately authorized, complete, and accurate
- Controls to provide reasonable assurance that erroneous input data are corrected and resubmitted
- Controls to provide reasonable assurance that output reports are reviewed by appropriate individuals for completeness and accuracy
- Controls to provide reasonable assurance that output received from the Organization is routinely reconciled to relevant user organization control totals

The list of user-organization control considerations presented above and those presented with certain specified control objectives do not represent a comprehensive set of all the controls that should be employed by user organizations. Other controls may be required at user organizations.

3

### Information Provided by the Service Auditor

> **Note to Readers:** SAS No. 70, *Service Organizations*, as amended, does not require that a service auditor describe tests of the control environment, risk assessment, monitoring, or information and communication. However, if a service auditor determines that describing tests of these components may be useful to user auditors, the service auditor may include such tests in the description of tests of operating effectiveness. This sample report does not include such information.

# Control Objectives, Related Controls, and Tests of Operating Effectiveness

## General Computer Controls

### Systems Development and Maintenance

*Control objective 1.* Controls provide reasonable assurance that changes to existing applications are authorized, tested, approved, properly implemented, and documented.

*Description of controls.* Each user organization designates the individuals who are authorized to request program changes. All program-change requests are submitted in writing to the manager of customer support. The manager of customer support maintains a log of all program-change requests received.

After a program-change request has been received and logged, it is reviewed by personnel in the customer support department to determine whether the requested change is an enhancement of a program or the correction of a programming error and to develop an estimate of the number of hours that will be required to make and implement the program change.

Biweekly management meetings are held with the director of information systems, the manager of application programming, and representatives of the user organizations to consider program-change requests and the status of active projects. Based on these discussions, the director of information systems approves or disapproves the change request. Upon approval, the director of information systems signs off on the program-change request and forwards it to the manager of application programming.

The manager of application programming receives approved program-change requests and prepares a customer work request (CWR) form. Information listed on the form includes the name of the originator, the name of the bank, the bank's user code, the program affected, and a description of the requested program change. A log of all CWRs is maintained and monitored by the manager of application programming.

The director of information systems must authorize change control personnel to release production-program source code to the programmer. The programming staff does not have direct access to production-program source code. The programmer makes changes to program code using a program-development library. The programmer does not have the ability to compile a changed program into executable form in the production environment. Programming changes are made using an online programming utility, and changes to source code are generated and annotated with the date of the change. Depending on the change, program unit tests and system tests are performed by the programmer and reviewed by the manager of application programming.

Acceptance tests are performed using test files, and the resulting output is verified by the requesting party. Recently processed production data is used as the test data, without updating any live files. If the program change involves a new function, test data is jointly developed by the programmer and the requesting party. All test results are verified by the programmer, the manager of application programming, and the requesting party. At the completion of all testing, the programmer, manager of application programming, and the requesting party sign off on the CWR.

After acceptance tests are completed, the director of information systems reviews all test results and documentation. If the director is satisfied with the program change, he or she authorizes change-control personnel to compile the new source code in the production environment and sign off on the CWR.

Updates to the production libraries are performed by change-control personnel after authorization by the director of information systems. Each time a program is compiled in the production environment, an entry is electronically recorded in a log that is printed and reviewed daily for any unauthorized activity.

Documentation is updated by the programmer, reviewed by the manager of application programming, and distributed to the appropriate parties.

*Tests of operating effectiveness.*

- Inspected documents evidencing the processing of program-change requests to determine whether requests are logged, reviewed by appropriate management personnel, and submitted in writing.

- Inspected the log of CWRs and traced a sample of entries to the CWR form and the corresponding program-change request. Inspected each CWR form and program-change request in the sample for completeness and proper approval. For the program changes in the sample that were completed and implemented during the period, inspected the test results for proper documentation and approval. Inspected the CWR forms for proper authorization of the program change to be compiled in the production environment.

- Selected a sample of program changes implemented during the period from a report generated by the program-change software and inspected the CWR form and program-change request for completeness and proper approval.

- Determined through review of various system reports, security tables, and observation that the programming staff does not have direct access to program-source code.

- Inspected a sample of the daily logs of compiled programs for reasonableness and evidence of review.

*Results of tests.* No exceptions were noted.

---

**Note to Readers:** The controls and tests of operating effectiveness for control objectives 2 through 9 are not presented in this sample report.

---

*Control objective 2.* Controls provide reasonable assurance that new applications being developed are authorized, tested, approved, properly implemented, and documented.

*Control objective 3.* Controls provide reasonable assurance that changes to the existing system software and implementation of new system software are authorized, tested, approved, properly implemented, and documented.

*Access*

*Control objective 4.* Controls provide reasonable assurance that physical access to computer equipment, storage media, and program documentation is restricted to properly authorized individuals.

*Control objective 5.* Controls provide reasonable assurance that logical access to system resources (for example, programs, data, tables, and parameters) is reasonable and restricted to properly authorized individuals.

### Computer Operations

*Control objective 6.* Controls provide reasonable assurance that processing is appropriately authorized and scheduled, and deviations from scheduled processing are identified and resolved.

*Control objective 7.* Controls provide reasonable assurance that data transmissions between Example Computer Service Organization and its user organizations are complete and accurate.

## Savings Application Controls

*Control objective 8.* Controls provide reasonable assurance that savings deposit and withdrawal transactions are received from authorized sources.

*Control objective 9.* Controls provide reasonable assurance that savings deposit and withdrawal transactions received from the user organizations are initially recorded completely and accurately.

*Control objective 10.* Controls provide reasonable assurance that programmed interest and penalties are calculated in conformity with the description.

---

**Note to Readers:** Control objective 10 illustrates a situation in which the application of a specific user-organization control is required to achieve the control objective. See "User Control Considerations" below and SAS No. 70, as amended (AU sec. 324.46).

---

*Description of controls.* Application security restricts update access to user-defined indexes, used to calculate interest and penalties, to the appropriate user organization. Within each user organization, passwords are required to update or change the indexes.

Programs used to calculate interest and penalties are subject to the controls described for control objective 1, "Controls provide reasonable assurance that changes to existing applications are authorized, tested, approved, properly implemented, and documented."

*User control considerations.* User organizations are responsible for establishing controls at the user organizations to restrict access to and change of user-defined indexes to authorized user-organization personnel. Any index can be selected and changed online at any time by user organizations with an appropriate password. The balances applicable to each rate are established by the user organizations in account-type parameters. A report can be generated that shows the current content of the indexes and the date they were last changed.

*Tests of operating effectiveness*

- Selected a sample of tables containing user-defined indexes for interest and penalty calculations. Inspected the application security tables to determine whether access to change entries in the indexes was restricted to the appropriate user organizations.
- Observed the process of changing indexes (using a test facility), noting that passwords are required.

**AAG-SRV APP A**

Changes to the interest and penalty calculation programs were included in the population of program changes tested for control objective 1.

*Results of tests.* No exceptions were noted.

> **Note to Readers:** The service auditor performs procedures to test the fairness of the presentation of the description of how interest and penalties are calculated and also performs procedures to test the operating effectiveness of the controls that provide reasonable assurance that programmed interest and penalties are calculated in conformity with the description. The nature and objective of the procedures performed to evaluate the fairness of the presentation of the description are different from those performed to evaluate the operating effectiveness of the controls. The service auditor might recalculate interest and penalties to test the fairness of the description; however, recalculation alone generally would not provide evidence of the operating effectiveness of the controls over the calculation of interest and penalties. In this example, the service auditor tested the general computer controls to obtain evidence related to the operating effectiveness of the controls because the service organization relies on the computer to calculate interest and penalties. The service auditor generally would not indicate that the only test of operating effectiveness performed for this control objective was recalculating interest and penalties.

> **Note to Readers:** The controls related to control objectives 11 through 13 are not presented in this sample report.

*Control objective 11.* Controls provide reasonable assurance that processing is performed in accordance with user specifications.

*Control objective 12.* Controls provide reasonable assurance that data maintained on files remain authorized, complete, and accurate.

*Control objective 13.* Controls provide reasonable assurance that output data and documents are complete and accurate and distributed to authorized recipients on a timely basis.

**4**

**Other Information Provided by Example Computer
Service Organization**

> **Note to Readers:** Details of other information provided by Example Computer Service Organization are not included in this sample report.

## Example 2

**Example Trust Organization,
Institutional Trust Division**

**Report on Controls Placed in Operation
and Tests of Operating Effectiveness**

**Table of Contents**

## Section Description of Section

**1.** Independent Service Auditor's Report

**AAG-SRV APP A**

**2.** Example Trust Organization's Description of Controls

Overview of Services Provided

Control Environment

> Organization
>
> Management Control
>
> Controls Related to Personnel
>
> Other Considerations
>
> Internal Audit

Risk Assessment

Monitoring

Information and Communication

> Description of Computerized Information Systems
>
> Description of Transaction Processing
>
> > Basic Trust and Custody Services
> >
> > Trade Execution
> >
> > Asset Custody and Control
> >
> > Income Accrual, Collections, and Corporate Actions
> >
> > Client Accounting
> >
> > Account Administration*
> >
> > Investment/Cash Management*
> >
> > Master Trust*
> >
> > Securities Lending*
> >
> > Contributions/Receipts*
> >
> > Benefit Payments/Distributions*
> >
> > Participant Recordkeeping*
> >
> > Customer Reporting*
>
> Communication With Customers*

Subservice Organizations

Control Objectives, Related Controls, and Service Auditor's Tests of Operating Effectiveness

> Transaction Processing
>
> Existence
>
> Computerized Information Systems*

User Control Considerations

**3.** Information Provided by the Service Auditor

*The description of the service auditor's tests of operating effectiveness and the results of those tests are presented in section 2 of this type 2 report, adjacent to the service organization's description of controls. The description of the tests of operating effectiveness and the results of those tests are the responsibility of the service auditor and should be considered information provided by the service auditor.*

---

* Items marked with an asterisk are presented in the table of contents for illustrative purposes only and are either included in part in or left entirely out of this illustrative type 2 report.

**AAG-SRV APP A**

1

### Independent Service Auditor's Report

To the Board of Directors of Example Trust Organization:

We have examined the accompanying description of the controls of Example Trust Organization's Institutional Trust Division. Our examination included procedures to obtain reasonable assurance about whether (1) the accompanying description presents fairly, in all material respects, the aspects of Example Trust Organization's controls that may be relevant to a user organization's internal control as it relates to an audit of financial statements; (2) the controls included in the description were suitably designed to achieve the control objectives specified in the description, if those controls were complied with satisfactorily, and user organizations and subservice organizations applied the controls contemplated in the design of Example Trust Organization's controls; and (3) such controls had been placed in operation as of December 31, 20XX. Example Trust Organization uses various service organizations to maintain custody and obtain prices of securities. The accompanying description includes only those controls and related control objectives of Example Trust Organization, and does not include controls and related control objectives of the custodial and pricing service organizations. Our examination did not extend to controls of the custodial and pricing service organizations. The control objectives were specified by the management of Example Trust Organization. Our examination was performed in accordance with standards established by the American Institute of Certified Public Accountants and included those procedures we considered necessary in the circumstances to obtain a reasonable basis for rendering our opinion.

In our opinion, the accompanying description of the controls of Example Trust Organization's Institutional Trust Division presents fairly, in all material respects, the relevant aspects of Example Trust Organization's controls that had been placed in operation as of December 31, 20XX. Also, in our opinion, the controls, as described, are suitably designed to provide reasonable assurance that the specified control objectives would be achieved if the described controls were complied with satisfactorily and user organizations and subservice organizations applied the controls contemplated in the design of Example Trust Organization's controls.

In addition to the procedures we considered necessary to render our opinion as expressed in the previous paragraph, we applied tests to specific controls to obtain evidence about their effectiveness in meeting the related control objectives during the period from January 1, 20XX, to December 31, 20XX. The specific controls, related control objectives, and the nature, timing, extent, and results of the tests are summarized on pages XX through XX of this report. This information has been provided to user organizations of Example Trust Organization's Institutional Trust Division and to their auditors to be taken into consideration, along with information about internal control at user organizations, when making assessments of control risk for user organizations. In our opinion the controls that were tested, as described on pages XX through XX, were operating with sufficient effectiveness to provide reasonable, but not absolute, assurance that the related control objectives specified on those pages were achieved during the period from January 1, 20XX, to December 31, 20XX. The relative effectiveness and significance of specific controls at Example Trust Organization and their effect on assessments of control risk at user organizations are dependent on their interaction with the controls and other factors present at individual user organizations. We have performed no procedures to evaluate the effectiveness of controls at individual user organizations.

The description of controls at Example Trust Organization is as of December 31, 20XX, and information about tests of the operating effectiveness of specific controls covers the period from January 1, 20XX, to December 31, 20XX. Any projection of such information to the future is subject to the risk that, because of change, the description may no longer portray the controls in existence. The potential effectiveness of specific controls at Example Trust Organization is subject to inherent limitations and, accordingly, errors or fraud may occur and not be detected. Furthermore, the projection of any conclusions, based on our findings, to future periods is subject to the risk that (1) changes made to the system or controls, (2) changes in processing requirements, or (3) changes required because of the passage of time may alter the validity of such conclusions.[3]

This report is intended solely for use by the management of Example Trust Organization, its users, and the independent auditors of its users.[4]

January 15, 20XX

2

**Example Trust Organization's
Description of Controls**

# Overview of Services Provided

Example Trust Organization (the Organization) is a full-service trust organization providing fiduciary services to corporate, personal, and institutional trust users. The Organization provides services through the following five divisions:

- *Corporate Trust Division.* Serves as a trustee for securities issued by corporations....

- *Personal Trust Division.* Services trusts established by individuals, foundations....

- *Institutional Trust Division.* Services institutional users, including employee benefit plans, public funds, insurance companies, and other financial institutions. The Institutional Trust Division has ultimate responsibility for the administration of institutional trust accounts (Accounts), including liaising with plan sponsors and investment managers. Account administration includes customer accounting and reporting, securities lending administration, participant loan administration, performance measurement, and compliance with the Employee Retirement Income Security Act (ERISA) of 1974. Each Account has a designated administrator in the Institutional Trust Division. The

---

[3] This sentence has been expanded to describe the risks of projecting any evaluation of the controls to future periods because of the failure to make needed changes to a system or controls, as provided for in Auditing Interpretation No. 5, "Statements About the Risk of Projecting Evaluations of the Effectiveness of Controls to Future Periods"of SAS No. 70, *Service Organizations*, as amended.

[4] SAS No. 87 (AU sec. 532.19c) presents the following illustrative restricted-use paragraph:
> This report is intended solely for the information and use of [the specified parties] and is not intended to be and should not be used by anyone other than these specified parties.

The language in that paragraph may be used in a service auditor's report.

administrator is supported by the Investment Management Division for accounts for which the Organization has investment discretion. The Institutional Trust Division is organized along regional lines, with a senior executive responsible for oversight of each region's activities. The senior executives report to the executive vice president of the Institutional Trust Division, who reports to the president of the Organization.

- *Investment Management Division.* Provides investment advisory services to accounts of the Corporate Trust, Personal Trust, and Investment Trust Divisions for which the Organization is granted investment discretion.

- *Trust Support Division.* Serves as a central utility for the processing of transactions for users of the Corporate Trust, Personal Trust, and Institutional Trust Divisions. The Trust Support Division is organized along functional lines and includes the following groups:

  — *Computerized information systems group (CISG).* Provides data processing services to the five divisions of the Organization. The CISG operates from a centralized processing site that provides numerous application-processing services to its users. The CISG's size and organization provide for separation of incompatible duties relating to computer operations, systems and programming, system software support, and data control. CISG personnel are subject to the Organization's personnel controls described on page XXX.

  — *Securities processing group.* Is responsible for securities movement and control, asset custody and control, securities lending, income accrual and collection, and corporate actions.

  — *Divisional support group.* Is responsible for liaising with the Institutional Trust Division and the other divisions.

  — *Benefit payment, disbursement, and participant recordkeeping group.*

# Control Environment

## Organization

Set forth in Figure 1 is the organization chart for Example Trust Organization at December 31, 20XX.

The Organization's trust activities are overseen by the Trust Committee of the Board of Directors. The Trust Committee has established the following committees to oversee the Organization's fiduciary activities relating to Accounts: Trust Policy Committee, Investment Committee, Administrative and Investment Review Committee, and Trust Real Estate Investment Committee. Each committee is charged with monitoring and establishing policy for the fiduciary activities under its oversight.

This report addresses the Institutional Trust Division, which directly services Accounts. It also addresses the Investment Management and Trust Support Divisions to the extent that these divisions support the activities of the Institutional Trust Division. Activities of the Corporate Trust and Personal Trust Divisions are beyond the scope of this report.

Trust activities are conducted in accordance with written policy and procedure guides that have been adopted by the trust policy committee. Policy and procedure guides are periodically updated. The responsibilities of the institutional trust and trust support divisions are allocated among personnel so as to segregate the following functions:

- Processing and recording transactions
- Maintaining custody of assets
- Reconciliation activities
- Compliance monitoring

**Figure 1**

**Organization Chart for Example Trust Organization**

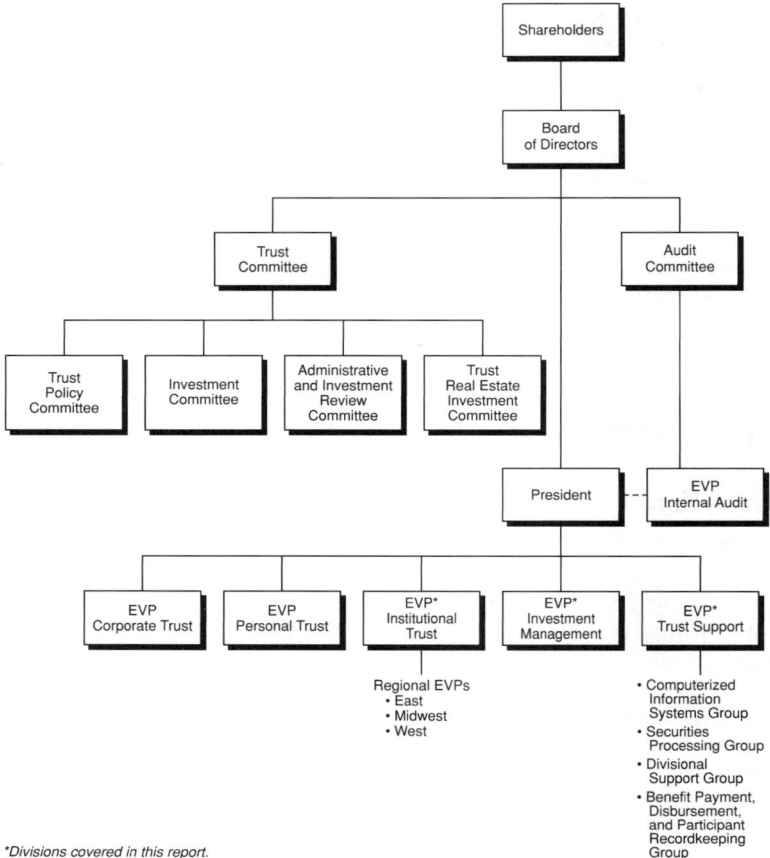

*Divisions covered in this report.

## Management Control

The Organization has a formal management information and reporting system that enables management to monitor key control and performance measurements.

Adherence to trust controls is monitored through a self-assessment program that is overseen by the compliance unit of the Institutional Trust Division. The assessment program has been designed to periodically evaluate Account administration and support operations for compliance with the Institutional Trust Division's authorizing document, the Organization's controls, and the applicable regulatory requirements. Results of the assessments are communicated to management and the trust committee.

## Controls Related to Personnel

The Organization has formal hiring practices designed to ensure that new employees are qualified for their job responsibilities. Each new-position hiring must be jointly approved by the human resources department and the manager of the department requiring the employee. Hiring policies include requiring that employees have minimum education and experience requirements, that written references be submitted, and that employees execute confidentiality statements. The Organization also performs background and credit investigations of potential employees.

Training of personnel is accomplished through supervised on-the-job training, outside seminars, and in-house classes. Certain positions require the completion of special training. For example, Account administrators are trained in ERISA rules and regulations. Department managers are responsible for ensuring that all Account administrators complete such training. Department managers are also responsible for encouraging the training and development of employees so that all personnel continue to qualify for their functional responsibilities.

Formal performance reviews are conducted on a periodic basis. Employees are evaluated on objective criteria based on performance. An overall rating (unsatisfactory, satisfactory, exceptional) is assigned.

## Other Considerations

The Organization's controls are documented in its corporate compliance manual (CCM). The CCM is organized by product and business unit and sets forth the Organization's controls, the laws and regulations to which the product or business unit is subject, and the compliance responsibilities of specific positions within the Organization.

The Organization has a formal conflict-of-interest policy that, among other things, establishes rules of conduct for employees who service Accounts. Employees and their immediate families are prohibited from divulging confidential information about client affairs, trading in securities of clients or their affiliates, and taking any action that is not in the best interest of clients. In addition, investment advisers in the Investment Management Division must provide periodic brokerage statements to a compliance officer who reviews the statements for transactions proscribed by Organization policy. Annually, each officer must confirm in writing his or her compliance with the Organization's conflict-of-interest policy.

The Organization is subject to regulation and supervision by the Office of the Comptroller of the Currency (OCC). Accordingly, the Organization is required to file periodic reports with the OCC and is subject to periodic examination by the OCC.

The Organization maintains insurance coverage against major risks. Insurance policies include an errors and omissions bond, employee fidelity bond, blanket-lost-original instruments bond, bankers' blanket bond, and trust-property-managers bond. Coverage is maintained at levels that the Organization considers reasonable given the size and scope of its operations, and is provided by insurance companies that Organization management believes are financially sound.

## Internal Audit

Trust activities are monitored by the internal audit group, which reports to the audit committee of the board of directors. The internal audit program is designed to evaluate compliance with the Organization's controls and the laws and regulations to which the Organization is subject, including ERISA. The program also addresses the soundness and adequacy of accounting, operating, and administrative controls. Internal audits cover four broad areas of fiduciary services: account administration, regulatory compliance, transaction accounting, and asset custody. Internal audits of asset custody include periodic verification of assets held in trust through physical examination, confirmation, or review of reconciliations and underlying source documents. Formal reports of audit findings are prepared and submitted to management and to the audit committee.

## Risk Assessment

The Organization has placed into operation a risk-assessment process to identify and manage risks that could affect the Organization's ability to provide reliable transaction processing to customers of the Institutional Trust Division. This process requires management to identify significant risks inherent in the processing of various types of transactions for customers and to implement appropriate measures to monitor and manage these risks.

This process has identified risks resulting from the nature of the services provided by the Institutional Trust Division, and management has implemented various measures designed to manage these risks. Risks identified in this process include:

- Operational risk associated with computerized information systems; manual processes involved in transaction processing; and external systems, for example, depository interfaces.
- Credit risk associated with, among other things, securities settlement; securities loans, and investment of related cash collateral.

- Market risk associated with the investment of cash collateral and the valuation of securities.
- Fiduciary risk associated with acting on behalf of customers.

Each of these risks is monitored as described under "Risk Monitoring," on page XXX of this report.

# Monitoring

The management and supervisory personnel of the Institutional Trust Division monitor performance quality and control operation as a normal part of their activities. The Organization has implemented a series of "key indicator" management reports that measure the results of various processes involved in providing transaction processing to customers. Key indicator reports include reports that identify:

- The name, age, and cause of differences noted in various reconciliations, such as Securities Movement and Control System (SMAC) versus Depository Trust Company (DTC), Depository Trust Company/Mortgage Backed Securities Division (DTC/MBS), and the Federal Reserve Bank (FED); accrued income versus amounts actually collected.
- The number of failed settlement transactions.
- Variances (or absence thereof) in the price of securities held by customers.
- Various computerized information system events, such as failed access attempts, rejected items, deviations from scheduled processing, and program changes.

These reports are periodically reviewed (depending on the nature of the item being reported on) by appropriate levels of management, and action is taken as necessary. Depending on the nature, age, and amount (as applicable) of processing exceptions, they are referred to succeedingly higher levels of management for review.

# Information and Communication

## Description of Computerized Information Systems[5]

- *Processing environment.* The CISG operates a large-scale computer facility that has two mainframe computers. One computer is primarily used to support application processing and the other is primarily used to support application maintenance, development, testing, and systems software maintenance and testing. The computers are supported by the manufacturer's operating system and related components....
- *Security/access.* The CISG has a centralized security administration department. This department is responsible for ensuring that the Organization adheres to corporate security policy that.... Access to

---

[5] In an actual report, there would be a more comprehensive description of the computer applications and the general computer controls. Such information is not included in this sample report.

system resources and production information and program files is protected from unauthorized users by a global-access control system that....

- *Application development / maintenance.* All requests for the development of new systems and changes to existing systems are submitted to the director of the CISG. All requests are processed within a software management system that includes the following processes: project request....

## Description of Transaction Processing

*Basic Trust and Custody Services*

Most of the transaction processing for Accounts is automated. Controls over access and changes to the automated systems are described in the section titled "Description of Computerized Information Systems." Set forth in Figure 2 is an overview of the Organization's applications, interfaces, and relationships to investment advisers, brokers, depositories, and custodians.

The application systems were developed by the Organization and are operated on the Organization's mainframe computer at its information center in New York City. The functions of each system are briefly described here:

- *Institutional delivery system (IDS).* Accepts automated trade inputs from terminals at outside investment advisers and investment management division advisers. Compares the trade inputs with broker trade notifications and interfaces with depositories or other custodians for trade delivery and settlement information, income collection, corporate actions, and security positions. Interfaces with the Organization's wire transfer system for payments and receipts related to security purchase and sale transactions, income receipts, and other cash transactions.

- *Security movement and control system (SMAC).* Maintains inventory records of the Organization's position in individual securities (including the physical location of such securities or the depository/custodian at which they are maintained) and the allocation of such positions to individual clients of the Organization, including, but not limited to, Accounts.

- *Automated income system (AIS).* Receives transmissions of dividend declarations from outside pricing and corporate action services. Computes interest accruals on fixed-income securities. Tracks and processes the receipt of income. Allocates income to individual clients of the Organization, including, but not limited to, Accounts.

- *Corporation action system (CAS).* Receives transmissions of corporate actions, such as stock splits, reorganizations, and mergers. Supports the process of notification of security holders of actions and decision follow-ups (in the case of nonmandatory actions, such as tender offers).

- *Trust accounting system (TAS).* Obtains the prices of security holdings from outside sources. Performs analytical testing of the reasonableness of prices. Maintains records for accounts and generates accounting statements.

**Figure 2**

**Transaction Processing of Accounts of Example Trust Organization**

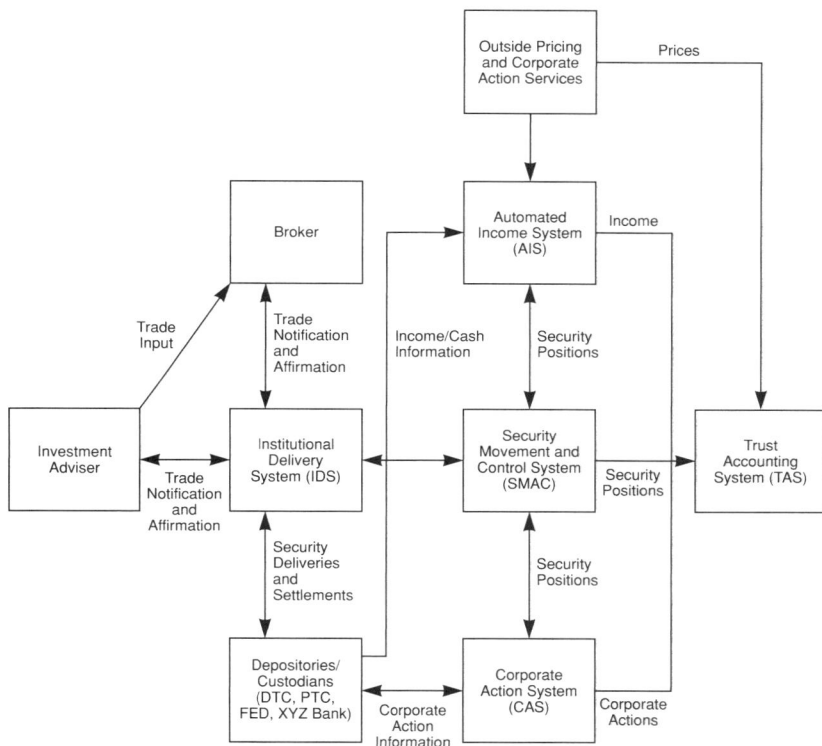

*Trade Execution*

Security trades are initiated by the Investment Management Division or by third-party advisers having investment discretion over particular Accounts. Trade information is input into the IDS via a terminal at the investment adviser. Nonautomated-trade-execution instructions (received via facsimile transmission [fax] or telephone) are authenticated by signature verification or call-back procedure and are input into the IDS by authorized personnel in the securities processing group. Trade information is confirmed in writing by the Organization with the broker/dealer who placed the trade.

Executed trades are affirmed through an automated process that compares the IDS trade information to trade depository information that the depository receives from the trade counterparty. The IDS provides for automated securities settlement on the prearranged date, which is typically three days after the trade date, or one day after the trade date for same day/next day settlements. Exceptions to the affirmation process are individually researched and resolved. Depositories include the DTC, the DTC/MBS, the FED, and XYZ Bank. Trade positions for settlement with outside depositories are reconciled daily and a net settlement is made with each depository.

Deliveries of securities (via depositories or via physical delivery of securities in the Organization's vault) in connection with security-sale transactions are effected only upon the receipt of cash. Similarly, cash is paid for security-purchase transactions only upon receipt of the securities. If the securities are not received or delivered on the settlement date, the settlement "fails." In that case, the purchase or sale of the security is reflected in the customer's portfolio, and a payable or receivable, respectively, is recorded for the future cash payment or receipt. The Organization monitors such fails through the IDS and the SMAC to ensure that they are resolved on a timely basis.

Free deliveries of securities are sometimes required for securities pledged as collateral or for reregistration. Free deliveries of collateral are initiated by the investment manager through ordinary trade input. Free deliveries for reregistration are typically physical (that is, not via a depository).

The Security Movement and Control Department of the Trust Support Division is responsible for the receipt and delivery of physical securities (other than purchase and sale transactions), the processing of maintenance entries, securities reregistration, and the transfer of securities between Accounts, as instructed by the account administrator. Securities are received via certified or registered mail. Hand-delivered securities are received under dual control. Securities being processed are maintained in a fireproof file that is secured in a vault during nonbusiness hours. Securities that must be delivered to external custodians are sent by insured courier. Receipt of the security is confirmed directly with the custodian. A log is maintained of all securities sent to a transfer agent for change of the nominee name. Follow-up is required if the security is not returned in 30 days. Mail-loss affidavits are prepared if the security is lost in transit to or from the transfer agent.

*Asset Custody and Control*

The Organization maintains trust assets at three depositories, one custodian bank, and in the Organization's vault in New York City. Custodial relationships are reviewed on a periodic basis to ensure that the quality and extent of services are adequate for the Organization's needs.

Assets are recorded on the SMAC by location code. Asset-holding lists can be provided on an asset, account, or location code level. Asset-holding lists are used by the Organization to prepare custodian reconciliations and to resolve any out-of-balance positions. Assets are recorded on the SMAC and identified to individual Accounts. Physical holdings of securities or book-entry holdings at depositories are held in aggregate under Example Trust Organization's name as trustee or nominee. Asset-holding lists provide detailed information by Account to permit the reconciliation of aggregate positions by security to the individual Account positions.

Reconciliations of asset positions between the DTC, the DTC/MBS, and the FED and the Organization's SMAC are performed on a daily basis. Reconciliations of asset positions between XYZ Bank and the Organization's SMAC are performed on a daily basis. The reconciliations are produced by comparing the custodian's position, per custodian-provided computer tapes, to the SMAC's asset-position listing. An aged exception report is produced that is used for follow-up. Reconciling items aged over 30 days are reported to senior management.

The trust vaults are maintained under dual control at all times. Securities placed into or removed from the vaults are recorded in vault logs. Any security removed from the vaults must be returned to the main vault or placed in a night vault at the end of each business day. Annual vault counts are performed by internal auditors on a surprise basis.

## Income Accrual, Collections, and Corporate Actions

The Income Accrual and Collection Department of the Securities Processing Group is responsible for processing and recording income accruals, collecting dividends and interest due on the payable date, processing income received, investigating underpayments and overpayments, and processing due bills and claims for income. Interest income is recorded to Accounts on an accrual basis. Discounts are accreted and premiums are amortized in accordance with customer instructions. Dividend income is recorded to Accounts on the ex-dividend date, as directed by the corporate actions department of the securities processing group.

Income collections, accruals, and cash dividends are processed using the AIS. Other corporate actions, such as tender offers and stock splits, are processed using the CAS. Both the AIS and the CAS receive data regarding corporate actions by independent sources. Information about trust-asset holdings of the Organization is obtained by the AIS and the CAS through an automated interface with the SMAC. The AIS reads the security-holdings files of the SMAC daily to identify securities for which dividends have been declared and to ensure that AIS files of fixed-income securities are complete and accurate. The AIS then prepares, by user, a file of expected-income collections or an "income map." These maps are matched against the paying agent's records before the expected payment date to research and correct any discrepancies before the payment date. For securities held at depositories, information on expected payments is received from the depositories and from an automated interface with the AIS. For securities held in the vault, a printout of the income map is generated by the AIS and manually compared to the paying agent's advice. Similarly, income collections are subsequently reconciled to the income maps in the AIS. Differences between actual and expected receipts are identified by the AIS, and an exception report is generated and used for investigation. Once differences are resolved, the income maps are adjusted, if necessary, and then released to the TAS. This release causes the collection to be reflected in each user's account.

On a daily basis, the AIS provides information on income accruals to the SMAC so that the customer accounting records can be automatically updated.

On a daily basis, the CAS prepares a list of new and pending corporate actions. For mandatory actions, such as bond calls or stock splits, CAS updates the SMAC, the TAS, and the AIS to ensure that subsequent security pricings, income payments, and other items are accurate. Nonmandatory actions, such as tender offers, are assigned to a client-service representative by the area supervisor. The client-service representative contacts the customer or investment manager to obtain instructions. The outstanding action is maintained on a "tickler file" within the CAS. As the deadline for the action approaches, the customer or investment manager is contacted at specified and increasingly shorter intervals. If no instructions are received by the day before the action is due, the matter is referred to the account administrator for resolution.

## Client Accounting

Periodic accounting statements are prepared for each Account by the TAS.

The TAS receives information on income and corporate actions affecting Accounts from interfaces with the SMAC, the AIS, and the CAS. Holdings of exchange-traded securities are recorded at market value in the accounting statements based on prices transmitted from independent pricing service organizations. If prices are received from more than one pricing service organization, the prices are compared and any significant deviations are investigated. Nonexchange-traded securities or other types of investments are valued....

## Subservice Organizations

The Organization uses industry-recognized subservice organizations to achieve operating efficiency and to obtain specific expertise. The Organization periodically reviews the quality of the subservice organizations' performance.

The following are the principal subservice organizations used by the Organization:

- Depositories and Subcustodians—In addition to the Organization's vaults, the Organization uses domestic depositories, such as the DTC and FED, to settle and safekeep customer assets.
- Pricing Services—The Organization uses multiple pricing services such as ... for customer asset valuation. Information from pricing services is primarily received electronically and interfaces with SMAC.
- Corporate Actions Services—The Organization uses multiple corporate action services such as ... to obtain corporate action events and dividend data. Corporate action information is obtained both automatically and manually.

## Control Objectives, Related Controls, and Service Auditor's Tests of Operating Effectiveness

This section presents the following information provided by the Organization:

- The control objectives specified by the management of the Organization
- The controls established and specified by the Organization to achieve the specified control objectives

Also included in this section is the following information provided by the service auditor:

- A description of the testing performed by the service auditor to determine whether the Organization's controls were operating with sufficient effectiveness to achieve specified control objectives. The service auditor determined the nature, timing, and extent of the testing performed.
- The results of the service auditor's tests of operating effectiveness.

---

**Note to Readers:** SAS No. 70, as amended, does not require that a service auditor describe tests of the control environment, risk assessment, monitoring, or information and communication. However, if the service auditor determines that describing tests of these components may be useful to user auditors, the service auditor may include such tests in the description of tests. This sample report does not include such information.

---

# Transaction Processing

*Control objective 1:* Controls provide reasonable assurance that investment purchases and sales are properly authorized.

| Controls Specified by Example Trust Organization | Testing Performed by the Service Auditor | Results of Tests |
|---|---|---|
| Only authorized users are able to input trades into the institutional delivery system (IDS). | Tested the logical access controls, as described in control objective X.† | See control objective X for the results of tests.† |
| | Tested the program change controls, as described in control objective Y.‡ | See control objective Y for the results of tests.‡ |
| Trades that are initiated via fax or telephone are authenticated by signature verification or callback. | Inspected a sample of fax source documentation for evidence of signature verification. Compared the input documentation with the IDS output. | No relevant exceptions were noted. |
| | For a sample of transactions, observed the performance of the callback procedure over five days. | No relevant exceptions were noted. |
| | Observed personnel in the securities processing group input transactions. | No relevant exceptions were noted. |

*Control objective 2:* Controls provide reasonable assurance that investment purchases and sales are recorded completely, accurately, and on a timely basis.

| Controls Specified by Example Trust Organization | Testing Performed by the Service Auditor | Results of Tests |
|---|---|---|
| The institutional delivery system (IDS) compares the trade information from the investment adviser with the trade notifications from the broker/dealer. Differences are identified by IDS and resolved on a timely basis. Items that are unresolved on a timely basis require review and approval by management. | Processed a sample of test purchase and sale transactions through the IDS to determine whether differences were properly identified by the system. The sample included matched and unmatched items. | No relevant exceptions were noted. |

*(continued)*

---

† This refers to a control objective that would include a description of the logical access controls, the tests of the controls, and the results of the tests. Such information is not included in this sample report.

‡ This refers to a control objective that would include a description of the program change controls, the tests of the controls, and the results of the tests. Such information is not included in this sample report.

| Controls Specified by Example Trust Organization | Testing Performed by the Service Auditor | Results of Tests |
|---|---|---|
| | Inspected a sample of IDS trade difference reports noting the number and age of differences reported. | Noted that the number and age of differences appeared reasonable and within the Organization's guidelines. |
| | Observed personnel in the execution of follow-up procedures to resolve trade differences. | The procedures observed were consistent with the written policy. No relevant exceptions were noted. |
| | To corroborate written evidential matter, made inquiries of the trade-settlement personnel regarding the procedures followed to resolve differences. | No relevant exceptions were noted. |
| | Made inquiries of the trade-settlement personnel regarding the operation of the procedures through December 31, 20XX. | No relevant exceptions were noted. |
| | Tested the program change controls, as described in control objective Y.[‡] | See control objective Y for the results of tests.[‡] |
| The IDS compares the trade affirmations received from outside depositories with the trade input information received from the investment adviser. Differences are identified by the IDS and resolved on a timely basis. | Processed a sample of test purchase and sale transactions through the IDS to determine whether exceptions are properly identified and reported by the IDS. The sample included matched and unmatched items. | No relevant exceptions were noted. |
| | Inspected a sample of IDS trade difference reports noting the number and age of the differences reported. | Noted that the number and age of the differences appeared reasonable and within the Organization's guidelines. |
| | Observed personnel in the execution of follow-up procedures to resolve trade differences. | The procedures observed were consistent with written policies. No relevant exceptions were noted. |

*(continued)*

| Controls Specified by Example Trust Organization | Testing Performed by the Service Auditor | Results of Tests |
|---|---|---|
| | Made inquiries of the trade settlement personnel regarding the operation of the procedures through December 31, 20XX. | No relevant exceptions were noted. |
| | Tested the program change controls, as described in control objective Y.[‡] | See control objective Y for the results of tests.[‡] |
| Security positions with the Depository Trust Company (DTC), the Depository Trust Company/Mortgage Backed Securities Division (DTC/MBS), and the FED are reconciled on a daily basis, and security positions with XYZ Bank are reconciled monthly. The reconciliations are performed through a tape-to-tape computer-matching process (SMAC versus IDS). A report listing balancing positions and out-of-balance positions is produced for review and follow-up (as described below). | Used CAT to match various system records used to create the system generated DTC, DTC/MBS and FED to SMAC security position reconciliation to assess its completeness and accuracy. | No relevant exceptions were noted. |
| | Determined whether changes had been made to the computer programs that affect the SMAC and IDS reconciliations. (The program source code for the SMAC and IDS reconciliation logic was reviewed and tested in 20XX.) | No changes were noted. |
| | Inspected the balancing report at December 31, 20XX, noting the number and age of the SMAC/IDS security position differences. | No relevant exceptions were noted in the review of the balancing report. Noted that the number and age of the differences appeared reasonable and within the Organization's guidelines. |
| | Tested the program change controls, as described in control objective Y.[‡] | See control objective Y for the results of tests.[‡] |

(*continued*)

| Controls Specified by Example Trust Organization | Testing Performed by the Service Auditor | Results of Tests |
|---|---|---|
| Corporate actions are monitored and identified on a timely basis and are recorded in the corporate action system (CAS). The CAS properly values and records corporate actions. | Observed the daily processing and made inquiries of the corporate-actions unit personnel regarding the CAS's ability to identify and process corporate actions and the third-party sources for corporate actions that are interfaced directly to CAS. | No relevant exceptions were noted. |
| | Used online testing to determine whether corporate action data feeds are received completely and accurately. | No relevant exceptions were noted. |
| | Tested the proper recording for a sample of corporate actions per the CAS and the trust accounting system (TAS) and the validity of the reported corporate actions. Selected corporate actions occurring on a sample of days during 20XX that had been recorded in business publications to ascertain whether they were properly recorded by the CAS. | No relevant exceptions were noted. |
| | Tested the program-change controls as described in control objective Y.[‡] | See control objective Y for the results of tests.[‡] |
| *Fixed-Income Securities* | | |
| Assets with regular or fixed payments, such as corporate and government bonds, are set up on the SMAC at the time of acquisition. The SMAC automatically passes information about such assets to the AIS. Only authorized personnel can set up securities on the SMAC at the time of acquisition. | For a sample of fixed-income security positions, compared the details of the security holdings (for example, coupon rate, maturity date, payment frequency and dates) per the SMAC to the AIS. | No relevant exceptions were noted. |

*(continued)*

| Controls Specified by Example Trust Organization | Testing Performed by the Service Auditor | Results of Tests |
|---|---|---|
| | For a sample of securities set up on the SMAC during 20XX, compared the details of the security holding per the SMAC with the offering prospectus or comparable external documentation noting agreement. | Noted that the payment date for X of the securities included in a XX-item sample was incorrectly stated on the SMAC. Resampled an additional XX items noting no exceptions. |
| . | Tested the logical access controls as described in control objective X.† | See control objective X for the results of tests.† |

*Control objective 3:* **Controls provide reasonable assurance that investment income is recorded accurately and timely.**

| Controls Specified by Example Trust Organization | Testing Performed by the Service Auditor | Results of Tests |
|---|---|---|
| The security movement and control system (SMAC) and the automated income system (AIS) security holdings are automatically compared daily and, if necessary, reconciled by authorized individuals. | Made inquiries of management regarding the reconciliation procedures and the exception-resolution process. | No relevant exceptions were noted. |
| | Observed the performance of the daily reconciliation procedures. | The procedures observed were consistent with management's description. |
| | Inspected a sample of reconciliations to assess the reasonableness, number, and age of the reconciling items. | No relevant exceptions were noted. |
| | Made inquiries of the income-collection personnel regarding the operation of the procedure through December 31, 20XX. | No relevant exceptions were noted. |
| The AIS accrues uncollected investment income and automatically passes the accrual information to the TAS. | For a sample of various types of securities, recalculated the income accruals at September 30, 20XX, and compared the accrual per the AIS to the accrual per the TAS. | No relevant exceptions were noted. |

*(continued)*

---

† See footnote † in *Control objective 1.*
‡ See footnote ‡ in *Control objective 1.*

**AAG-SRV APP A**

| Controls Specified by Example Trust Organization | Testing Performed by the Service Auditor | Results of Tests |
|---|---|---|
| | Tested the program change controls as described in control objective Y.[‡] | See control objective Y for the results of tests.[‡] |
| _Equity Securities_ | | |
| To properly record income on equity securities, a computer tape of dividends declared is prepared and transmitted to the AIS by an outside service on a daily basis. The computer tape of securities reporting dividends for the day is compared with asset holdings on the SMAC, and anticipated dividend maps are created by the AIS. | Made inquiries of the income-collection personnel regarding the source of daily dividend tapes and the procedures followed to interface with the SMAC and the AIS. Observed the daily processing. | No relevant exceptions were noted. |
| | For a sample of equity securities, determined whether dividends declared were properly reflected in the AIS. | No relevant exceptions were noted. |
| | Tested the controls over data transmission, as described in control objective Z. [‖] | See control objective Z for the results of tests.[‖] |
| Dividend income is credited to the customer on the ex-dividend date. | Selected a sample of dividends per the AIS and verified that they were recorded in the TAS on the ex-date. | No relevant exceptions were noted. |

**Control objective 4:** Controls provide reasonable assurance that investment income is collected on a timely basis.

| Controls Specified by Example Trust Organization | Testing Performed by the Service Auditor | Results of Tests |
|---|---|---|
| The AIS compares the income received from the depository or directly from the issuer to the anticipated income map on a security-by-security basis. Differences between the expected receipts and the actual receipts are reported, investigated, and resolved by authorized income-collection personnel on a timely basis. | Processed a sample of test collections and corrections through the AIS to determine the propriety of the AIS income exception report. | No relevant exceptions were noted. |

(_continued_)

---

[‡] See footnote ‡ in _Control objective 1._

[‖] This refers to a control objective that would include a description of the data transmission controls, the tests of the controls, and the results of the tests. Such information is not included in this sample report.

**AAG-SRV APP A**

| Controls Specified by Example Trust Organization | Testing Performed by the Service Auditor | Results of Tests |
|---|---|---|
| | Inspected the anticipated income reports noting whether the nature and age of the outstanding differences were reasonable and within Organization guidelines. | No relevant exceptions were noted. |
| | Made inquiries of the income-collection personnel regarding the operation of the procedure through December 31, 20XX. | No relevant exceptions were noted. |
| | Observed the income-collection personnel investigating unresolved differences. | No relevant exceptions were noted. |
| | Tested the program change controls as described in control objective Y.[‡] | See control objective Y for the results of tests.[‡] |

***Control objective 5:*** **Controls provide reasonable assurance that the market value of exchange-traded securities is properly calculated using prices obtained from outside pricing services.**

| Controls Specified by Example Trust Organization | Testing Performed by the Service Auditor | Results of Tests |
|---|---|---|
| Daily transmissions of prices of exchange-traded securities are received from independent sources. | Made inquiries of the Organization's personnel regarding the sources of prices for various kinds of securities (for example, governments, corporate bonds, equities, asset-backed) and the procedures followed for the transmission and verification of prices. Observed the daily processing. | No relevant exceptions were noted. |
| | Tested the controls over data transmission, as described in control objective Z.[‖] | See control objective Z for the results of tests.[‖] |

*(continued)*

[‡] See footnote ‡ in *Control objective 1.*

| Controls Specified by Example Trust Organization | Testing Performed by the Service Auditor | Results of Tests |
|---|---|---|
| Market prices obtained from independent sources are automatically compared daily to assess the reasonableness of the prices received. Discrepancies in the prices are identified, researched, and resolved by authorized personnel. | Market prices obtained from independent sources are automatically compared daily to assess the reasonableness of the prices received. Discrepancies in the prices are identified, researched, and resolved by authorized personnel. | No relevant exceptions were noted. |
| Market prices are multiplied by the holdings in each customer's account on SMAC to determine the market value of the positions. | Used the CAT to recalculate the market value of the securities based on information provided by independent sources and the information contained on the SMAC. | No relevant exceptions were noted. |

## Existence

***Control objective 6:*** **Controls provide reasonable assurance that physically held securities are protected from loss, misappropriation, and unauthorized use.**

| Controls Specified by Example Trust Organization | Testing Performed by the Service Auditor | Results of Tests |
|---|---|---|
| Vaulted securities are physically inspected (or, in the case of a vault receipt, confirmed with the third party) on a cyclical basis by operations staff not involved in maintaining the vault. Annually, internal audit performs a full inspection or confirmation of vault securities and receipts. Securities inspected or receipts confirmed are compared to the SMAC records and differences are investigated. All inspections are conducted on a surprise basis. | Inspected or confirmed selected vault securities and receipts on September 8, 20XX, and compared to SMAC records. Reviewed the results of periodic inspections by operations staff and internal audit. | No relevant exceptions noted. |

*(continued)*

---

‖ See footnote ‖ in *Control objective 3.*

*Control objective 7*: Controls provide reasonable assurance that the entity's records accurately reflect securities held by third parties.

| Controls Specified by Example Trust Organization | Testing Performed by the Service Auditor | Results of Tests |
|---|---|---|
| For depository-eligible securities, SMAC security positions are automatically reconciled to depository records on a regular basis. Differences are identified, researched, and resolved on a timely basis by personnel not involved in transaction initiation or processing. Reconciliations and adjustments are subject to supervisory review. The volume by type and age of outstanding reconciling items are reported to management on a weekly basis. | Reperformed, using CAT, the automatic depository reconciliations and the preparation of the weekly management report regarding reconciliations. | No relevant exceptions noted. |
| | Reviewed a selection of management reports for evidence that items are timely reported to management. | No relevant exceptions noted. |
| | Inspected a sample of reconciling items to ascertain whether they were researched and resolved on a timely basis. | No relevant exceptions noted. |
| Non-depository-eligible securities are maintained in the vault. Vault access is physically restricted. Access to the vault requires the presence, at all times, of two authorized individuals; all such authorized individuals are not otherwise involved in transaction processing. | Observed the process by which dual control over and restricted access to the vault is maintained. | No relevant exceptions noted. |

**Note to Readers:** The control objectives included in this sample report are presented for illustrative purposes only and are not intended to represent a complete set of control objectives. Controls objectives 1 through 6 and the related controls presented on the preceding pages cover certain aspects of transaction processing. Other control objectives related to transaction processing and control objectives related to CIS that might need to be included in an actual report are not illustrated in this sample report.

# User Control Considerations

The Organization's processing of transactions and the controls over the processing were designed with the assumption that certain controls would be placed in operation at user organizations. This section describes some of the controls that should be in operation at user organizations to complement the controls at the Organization. User auditors should determine whether user organizations have established controls to ensure that:

- Instructions and information provided to the Organization from institutional trust users are in accordance with the provisions of the servicing agreement, trust agreement, or other applicable governing agreements or documents between the Organization and the user.

- Physical and logical access to the Organization's systems via terminals at user locations are restricted to authorized individuals.

- Timely written notification of changes to the plan, its objectives, participants, and investment managers is adequately communicated to the Organization.

- Timely written notification of changes in the designation of individuals authorized to instruct the Organization regarding activities, on behalf of the institutional trust user, is adequately communicated to the Organization.

- Timely review of reports provided by the Organization of institutional trust account balances and related activities is performed by the institutional trust user, and written notice of discrepancies is provided to the Organization.

- Timely written notification of changes in related parties for purposes of identifying parties-in-interest transactions is adequately communicated to the Organization.

3

**Information Provided by the Service Auditor**

The description of the service auditor's tests of operating effectiveness and the results of those tests are presented in section 2 of this report, adjacent to the service organization's description of controls. The description of the tests of operating effectiveness and the results of those tests are the responsibility of the service auditor and should be considered information provided by the service auditor.

# Appendix B

# *Illustrative Representation Letter for a Service Auditor's Engagement*

[*Date*]

To [*Name of Service Auditor*]

In connection with your engagement to report on Example Computer Service Organization's (the Organization) description of controls placed in operation and tests of operating effectiveness, we recognize that obtaining representations from us concerning the information contained in this letter is a significant procedure in enabling you to form an opinion on whether the description presents fairly, in all material respects, the relevant aspects of the Organization's controls that had been placed in operation as of [*specify date*], and whether the controls were suitably designed to provide reasonable assurance that the specified control objectives would be achieved if those controls were complied with satisfactorily (and whether the controls that were tested were operating with sufficient effectiveness to provide reasonable, but not absolute, assurance that the related control objectives were achieved for the [*specify the period covered by the tests of operating effectiveness*]).[1] Accordingly, we make the following representations, which are true to the best of our knowledge and belief.

**General**

We recognize that, as members of management of the Organization, we are responsible for the fair presentation of the description of the Organization's controls and for establishing and maintaining appropriate controls related to the processing of transactions for user organizations.

We believe that the description of controls presents fairly, in all material respects, those aspects of the Organization's controls that may be relevant to user organizations' internal control.

We have responded fully to all inquiries made to us by you during your examination.

**Description of Controls Placed in Operation**

The control objectives specified in our description of controls include all of the control objectives that we believe are relevant to users of the services described in this report and are appropriate based on the services provided to user organizations [or based on third-party criteria].

The controls described in the description of controls had been placed in operation as of [*specify date*].

---

[1] Included only when reporting on the operating effectiveness of controls to achieve specified control objectives.

The controls are suitably designed to achieve the control objectives specified in the description of controls.

We have disclosed to you any significant changes in controls that have occurred since the Organization's last examination [or "within the last 12 months" for initial examinations].

We have disclosed to you all design deficiencies in controls of which we are aware, including those for which we believe the cost of corrective action may exceed the benefits.

### Operating Effectiveness of Controls [2]

We have disclosed to you all instances of which we are aware of controls not operating with sufficient effectiveness to achieve specified control objectives.

### Illegal Acts, Fraud, or Uncorrected Error

We are not aware of any illegal acts, fraud, or uncorrected errors attributable to management or employees of the Organization who have significant roles relevant to the processing performed for user organizations.[3]

We understand that your examination was conducted in accordance with generally accepted auditing standards as defined and described by the American Institute of Certified Public Accountants and was, therefore, designed primarily for the purpose of expressing an opinion on (1) the Organization's description of controls, (2) the suitability of the design of the controls, [and (3) the operating effectiveness of the controls[4]], as described in the first paragraph of this letter, and that your procedures were limited to those that you considered necessary for this purpose.

Very truly yours,

[*Signature of appropriate service organization personnel*]

The letter of representation should be dated as of the completion of fieldwork.

---

[2] Included only when reporting on the operating effectiveness of controls to achieve specified control objectives.

[3] If there are such matters, management should include a representation as to whether the illegal acts, fraud, or uncorrected errors are clearly inconsequential. If such matters are not clearly inconsequential, management should include a representation that such matters have been communicated to the affected organizations.

[4] Included only when reporting on the operating effectiveness of controls to achieve specified control objectives.

# Appendix C

## Responsibilities of Service Organizations, Service Auditors, and User Auditors If Subservice Organizations Perform Significant Functions for User Organizations and Control Objectives Are Established by the Service Organization

| Service Organization's Responsibilities | Service Auditor's Responsibilities | User Auditor's Responsibilities |
|---|---|---|
| Describe the service organization's controls that may be relevant to user organizations' internal control (Statement on Auditing Standards [SAS] No. 70, *Service Organizations*, as amended [AICPA, *Professional Standards*, vol. 1, AU sec. 324.26]).

Describe the control objectives established by the service organization (SAS No. 70, as amended [AU sec. 324.34a]).

Identify the functions and nature of the processing performed by the subservice organization, and either: | Disclose in the service auditor's report that the control objectives were established by the service organization (SAS No. 70, as amended [AU sec. 324.29c and .44c]). The service auditor should be satisfied that the control objectives, as set forth by the service organization, are reasonable in the circumstances and consistent with the service organization's contractual obligations (SAS No. 70, as amended [AU sec. 324.35]).

Opine on (1) the fairness of the presentation of the description of controls placed in operation, (2) whether the controls were suitably designed to achieve specified control objectives [and, when the report includes tests of operating effectiveness, (3) whether the controls that were tested were operating with sufficient effectiveness to achieve the related control objectives], and either: | Determine whether the report meets the user auditor's needs. If the user auditor requires further information about the functions performed by the subservice organization or about the subservice organization's controls, the user auditor should consider obtaining information about the subservice organization in a manner similar to that described in SAS No. 70, as amended (AU sec. 324.07–.21). |

*(continued)*

**AAG-SRV APP C**

| Service Organization's Responsibilities | Service Auditor's Responsibilities | User Auditor's Responsibilities |
|---|---|---|
| *Carve-Out Method* 1 | *Carve-Out Method* | |
| 1. Omit from the description the subservice organization's relevant controls and control objectives and state in the description that the controls and control objectives have been omitted. | 1. Modify the scope paragraph of the service auditor's report to briefly summarize the functions and the nature of the processing performed by the subservice organization and to indicate that the relevant controls and control objectives of the subservice organization were omitted from the description. | |
| or | or | |
| *Inclusive Method* 1 | *Inclusive Method* | |
| 2. Include the subservice organization's relevant controls and control objectives in the description. The control objectives will include all of the objectives a user auditor would expect both the service organization and the subservice organization to achieve. | 2. Identify the entities included in the scope of the examination. With respect to the controls of the subservice organization, follow procedures comparable to those described in SAS No. 70, as amended (AU sec. 324.12), which include: <br><br> • Performing procedures related to the service organization's controls over the activities of the subservice organization. <br><br> • Performing procedures at the subservice organization. | |

1 This Guide does not provide for the option of having a service auditor make reference to or rely on a subservice auditor's report as the basis, in part, for the service auditor's opinion.

# Appendix D

## Responsibilities of Service Organizations, Service Auditors, and User Auditors If Subservice Organizations Perform Significant Functions for User Organizations and Control Objectives Are Established by an Outside Party

| Service Organization's Responsibilities | Service Auditor's Responsibilities | User Auditor's Responsibilities |
| --- | --- | --- |
| Describe the service organization's controls that may be relevant to user organizations' internal control (SAS No. 70, as amended [AU sec. 324.26]).<br><br>Describe the control objectives established by the outside party (SAS No. 70, as amended [AU sec. 324.34*a*]).<br><br>Identify the functions and nature of the processing performed by the subservice organization, and either: | Identify in the service auditor's report the source of the control objectives (SAS No. 70, as amended [AU sec. 324.29*c* and .44*c*.]). The service auditor does not need to determine whether the control objectives are reasonable in the circumstances and consistent with the service organization's contractual obligations because the control objectives have been established by an outside party (SAS No. 70, as amended [AU sec. 324.35]).<br><br>Opine on (1) the fairness of the presentation of the description of controls placed in operation, (2) whether the controls were suitably designed to achieve specified control objectives [and, when the report includes tests of operating effectiveness, (3) whether the controls that were tested were operating with sufficient effectiveness to achieve the related control objectives], and either: | Determine whether the report meets the user auditor's needs. If the user auditor requires further information about the functions performed by the subservice organization or about the subservice organization's controls, the user auditor should consider obtaining information about the subservice organization in a manner similar to that described in SAS No. 70, as amended (AU sec. 324.07–.21). |

| Service Organization's Responsibilities | Service Auditor's Responsibilities | User Auditor's Responsibilities |
|---|---|---|
| _Carve-Out Method_ 1 | _Carve-Out Method_ | |
| 1. Omit from the description the subservice organization's relevant controls and state in the description that these controls have been omitted. | 1. Modify the scope paragraph of the service auditor's report to briefly summarize the functions and the nature of the processing performed by the subservice organization and to indicate that the controls and related control objectives of the subservice organization are omitted from the description. | |
| or | or | |
| _Inclusive Method_ | _Inclusive Method_ | |
| 2. Include in the description the controls that the subservice organization is responsible for. 1 | 2. Identify the entities included in the scope of the examination. With respect to the controls of the subservice organization, follow procedures comparable to those described in SAS No. 70, as amended (AU sec. 324.12), which include: <br><br> • Performing procedures related to the service organization's controls over the activities of the subservice organization. <br><br> • Performing procedures at the subservice organization. | |

---

1 This Guide does not provide for the option of having a service auditor make reference to or rely on a subservice auditor's report as the basis, in part, for the service auditor's opinion.

# Appendix E

# *Illustrative Control Objectives for Various Types of Service Organizations* [1]

## Information Systems

The following illustrative information technology (IT) control objectives may be applicable to any service organization that uses IT in providing services that are part of a user organization's information system. They should be considered in addition to the illustrative control objectives that are applicable to specific types of service organizations.

Controls provide reasonable assurance that:

- New applications being developed are authorized, tested, approved, properly implemented, and documented.
- Changes to existing applications are authorized, tested, approved, properly implemented, and documented.
- Changes to the existing system software and implementation of new system software are authorized, tested, approved, properly implemented, and documented.
- Physical access to computer equipment, storage media, and program documentation is restricted to properly authorized individuals.
- Logical access to system resources (for example, programs, data, tables, and parameters) is restricted to properly authorized individuals.
- Processing is appropriately authorized and scheduled and that deviations from scheduled processing are identified and resolved.
- Data transmissions between the service organization and its user organizations are complete and accurate.

## Investment Adviser

The control objectives included in this section would be appropriate for an investment adviser who performs some or all of the following functions.

- Initiating and executing purchase and sale transactions, either by specific direction from the client or under discretionary authority granted by the client
- Determining whether transactions comply with guidelines and restrictions
- Reconciling records of security transactions and portfolio holdings, for each client, to statements received from the custodian
- Reporting to the customer on portfolio performance and activities

---

[1] This appendix does not include controls that might be required by regulatory agencies.

## Illustrative Control Objectives for an Investment Adviser

Controls provide reasonable assurance that:

- Investment guidelines and restrictions are established and monitored.
- Securities transactions and portfolio holdings are monitored for compliance with client guidelines and regulatory requirements, and are managed in accordance with investment objectives.
- Portfolio security purchase and sale transactions are appropriately authorized.
- Portfolio security purchase and sale transactions are executed timely and accurately.
- The cost of securities purchased and the proceeds of securities sold are accurately allocated among client accounts in accordance with company policy.
- Client account transactions and cash and security positions are completely and accurately recorded and settled in a timely manner.
- Securities are valued using current prices obtained from sources authorized by the customer.
- Controls provide reasonable assurance that investment income is accurately recorded in the proper period.
- Investment management fees and other account expenses are accurately calculated and recorded.
- Corporate actions are identified, processed, and recorded accurately and timely.

# Securities Custodian and Servicer

The control objectives in this section would be appropriate for a securities holder (custodian) and servicer that performs some or all of the following functions:

- Maintaining custody of securities and records of the securities held for the entities (Such securities may exist in physical or electronic form.)
- Collecting dividend and interest income and distributing such income to the entities
- Receiving notification of corporate actions and reflecting such actions in the records of entities
- Receiving notification of security purchase and sale transactions on behalf of entities for which the custodian is holding securities, and reflecting such transactions in the records of the entities
- Receiving payments from purchasers and disbursing proceeds to sellers for security purchase and sale transactions

## Illustrative Control Objectives for a Securities Custodian and Servicer

Controls provide reasonable assurance that:

- Changes to nonmonetary participant data (for example, address changes and changes in allocation instructions) are authorized and correctly recorded on a timely basis.

- Trades are authorized, recorded, settled, and reported completely, accurately, and timely and in accordance with the client agreement.
- Investment income is collected and recorded accurately and timely.
- Corporate actions are identified, processed, settled, and recorded accurately and timely.
- The market values of securities are calculated based on market prices obtained from authorized pricing sources.
- Cash receipts and disbursements are authorized, processed, and recorded completely, accurately, and timely.
- Physically-held securities are protected from loss, misappropriation, and unauthorized use.
- The entity's records accurately reflect securities held by third parties, for example, depositories or subcustodians.
- Lender and borrower participation in lending programs is authorized.
- Loan initiation, processing, maintenance, and termination are recorded accurately and timely.
- Loans are adequately collateralized, and collateral is recorded timely and accurately.
- Collateral is invested in accordance with the lender agreement and income is calculated and distributed accurately and timely.

# Participant Recordkeeper for Defined Contribution Plans

The illustrative control objectives included in this section would be appropriate for a participant recordkeeper for defined contribution plans that perform some or all of the following functions.

- Maintaining records of participant and employer contributions, disbursements, and account balances based on information received from the plan sponsor, participant, mutual fund investment adviser, transfer agent, custodian and others.
- Receiving instructions from participants and plan sponsors regarding investment elections, distributions, loans, hirings, terminations, and other matters, and communicating these instructions to other service organizations, such as transfer agents and custodians responsible for executing these instructions.
- Performing valuations of participant accounts and transactions.
- Periodic reporting to participants and plan sponsors.

## Illustrative Control Objectives for Participant Recordkeepers for Defined Contribution Plans

Controls provide reasonable assurance that:

- New accounts are properly established in the system in accordance with the plan agreement and individual elections.
- Changes to nonmonetary participant data (for example, address changes and changes in allocation instructions) are authorized and correctly recorded on a timely basis.
- Cash receipt transactions, loans, distributions of plan assets, and transactions reflecting a transfer of participants' funds among

investment options are recorded accurately, timely, and in accordance with instructions received from plan sponsors or participants.

- Investment income (loss) is accurately and timely allocated and recorded to individual participant accounts.
- Transactions and participant account balances are valued based on market prices obtained from authorized pricing sources.
- Participant transaction confirmations, and participant account statements, are accurate, distributed timely, and mailed directly to participants without intervention by individuals responsible for processing transactions.

## Portfolio Accountant

The illustrative control objectives in this section would be appropriate for a portfolio accountant that performs some or all of the following services for entities such as mutual funds.

- Maintaining records of securities, cash, and other portfolio assets based on information received from the plan sponsor, investment adviser, transfer agent, custodian and others.
- Performing valuations of portfolio assets and determining net asset values (aggregate and per unit).
- Periodic reporting to plan sponsors, investment advisers, and others.

### Illustrative Control Objectives for a Portfolio Accountant

Controls provide reasonable assurance that:

- Portfolio transactions are authorized, and processed and settled accurately and timely.
- Securities costs are accurately calculated and recorded.
- Portfolio securities are valued using current prices obtained from sources authorized by the customer.
- Investment income is accurately and timely calculated, and recorded.
- Corporate actions are processed completely, accurately, and timely.
- Expenses are accurately calculated, and recorded in accordance with the customer's instructions.
- The entity's capital stock (unit) activity is recorded completely, accurately, and timely.
- Dividend distribution rates are authorized and dividend amounts are timely and accurately calculated and recorded.
- Net asset value is accurately calculated.

## Transfer Agent

A transfer agent may perform a transfer function, registrar function, or both. The transfer function includes:[2]

- Canceling old certificates that are properly presented and endorsed in good deliverable form (which usually includes a signature guarantee).

---

[2] Source: AICPA Audit and Accounting Guide *Brokers and Dealers in Securities*.

- Making appropriate adjustments to the issuer's shareholder records.
- Establishing a new account and issuing new certificates in the name of the new owner.
- Reviewing legal documents to ensure that they are complete and in perfect order before transferring the securities.
- If the legal documents are incomplete, notifying the presenter that the documents are incomplete and holding the old certificate and accompanying documentation until the presenter sends the transfer agent the proper documents or rejecting the transfer and returning the securities.

The registrar function includes:

- Monitoring the issuance of securities in an issue to prevent the unauthorized issuance of securities.
- Ensuring that the issuance of the securities will not cause the authorized number of shares in an issue to be exceeded and that the number of shares represented by the new certificates corresponds to the number of shares on the canceled ones.
- Countersigning the certificate, after performing the functions listed above.

In addition to the functions of a transfer agent, a transfer agent that processes for mutual funds is also responsible for:

- Recording the amount of securities purchased by a shareholder on the issuer's books and redeeming (liquidating) shares upon receipt of the customer's written or wire request.
- Maintaining records of the name and address of each security holder, the amount of securities owned by each security holder, the certificate numbers corresponding to a security holder's position, the issue date of the security certificate, and the cancellation date of the security certificate.
- For many transfer agents, acting as paying agent for cash dividends and distributions of stock dividends and stock splits.

The following set of control objectives are applicable depending on the functions performed.

## Illustrative Control Objectives for a Transfer Agent

Controls provide reasonable assurance that:

- Transactions and adjustments, including as-of transactions, are authorized, processed accurately and timely, and valued at proper dollar and share amounts.
- Dividend and distribution rates are authorized, and dividend and distribution amounts are accurately and timely calculated and recorded.
- Transactions and adjustments are authorized and processed accurately.
- Fund distributions are properly recorded in shareholder accounts and are properly updated to the system.
- Tax withholdings are properly calculated, recorded and remitted.

- Shareholder account maintenance transactions are properly authorized and recorded and accurately and timely recorded.
- The master security file, the detail security holder file, and the authorized share total records are accurately maintained.
- Securities in the custody or possession of the transfer agent are protected from loss, misappropriation, or unauthorized use.
- Transfer-agent records accurately reflect cash held by third parties.
- Checks and certificates issued are authorized and timely and accurately recorded.
- Lost and stolen certificates are recorded timely and accurately.

# Appendix F

# *AICPA Professional Standards, AU Section 324: Service Organizations* [*]

(Supersedes SAS No. 44)

Sources: SAS No. 70; SAS No. 78; SAS No. 88; SAS No. 98.

See section 9324 **for interpretations of this section.**

**Effective for service auditors' reports dated after March 31, 1993, unless otherwise indicated.**

## Introduction and Applicability

.01   This section provides guidance on the factors an independent auditor should consider when auditing the financial statements of an entity that uses a service organization to process certain transactions. This section also provides guidance for independent auditors who issue reports on the processing of transactions by a service organization for use by other auditors.[1]

.02   For purposes of this section, the following definitions apply:

- *User organization*—The entity that has engaged a service organization and whose financial statements are being audited

- *User auditor*—The auditor who reports on the financial statements of the user organization

- *Service organization*—The entity (or segment of an entity) that provides services to a user organization that are part of the user organization's information system

- *Service auditor*—The auditor who reports on controls of a service organization that may be relevant to a user organization's internal control as it relates to an audit of financial statements

- *Report on controls placed in operation*—A service auditor's report on a service organization's description of its controls that may be relevant to a user organization's internal control as it relates to an audit of financial statements, on whether such controls were suitably designed to achieve specified control objectives, and on whether they had been placed in operation as of a specific date

- *Report on controls placed in operation and tests of operating effectiveness*—A service auditor's report on a service organization's description of its controls that may be relevant to a user organization's

---

[*]   Title amended, effective December 1999, by Statement on Auditing Standards No. 88.

[1]   For issuers, SAS No. 70 has been amended by PCAOB Release 2004-008. The following note is added after paragraph 1:
When performing an integrated audit of financial statements and internal control over financial reporting, refer to paragraphs B18-B29 of Appendix B, "Additional Performance Requirements and Directions; Extent-of-Testing Examples," in PCAOB Auditing Standard No. 2 regarding the use of service organizations.
[Footnote added as part of the 2005 conforming changes to this edition of the Guide. This footnote is not included in AU section 324 of AICPA *Professional Standards*.]

internal control as it relates to an audit of financial statements,[2] on whether such controls were suitably designed to achieve specified control objectives, on whether they had been placed in operation as of a specific date, and on whether the controls that were tested were operating with sufficient effectiveness to provide reasonable, but not absolute, assurance that the related control objectives were achieved during the period specified.

[Revised, April 2002, to reflect conforming changes necessary due to the issuance of Statement on Auditing Standards No. 94.]

.03 The guidance in this section is applicable to the audit of the financial statements of an entity that obtains services from another organization that are part of its information system. A service organization's services are part of an entity's information system if they affect any of the following:

- The classes of transactions in the entity's operations that are significant to the entity's financial statements
- The procedures, both automated and manual, by which the entity's transactions are initiated, recorded, processed, and reported from their occurrence to their inclusion in the financial statements
- The related accounting records, whether electronic or manual, supporting information, and specific accounts in the entity's financial statements involved in initiating, recording, processing and reporting the entity's transactions
- How the entity's information system captures other events and conditions that are significant to the financial statements
- The financial reporting process used to prepare the entity's financial statements, including significant accounting estimates and disclosures

Service organizations that provide such services include, for example, bank trust departments that invest and service assets for employee benefit plans or for others, mortgage bankers that service mortgages for others, and application service providers that provide packaged software applications and a technology environment that enables customers to process financial and operational transactions. The guidance in this section may also be relevant to situations in which an organization develops, provides, and maintains the software used by client organizations. The provisions of this section are not intended to apply to situations in which the services provided are limited to executing client organization transactions that are specifically authorized by the client, such as the processing of checking account transactions by a bank or the execution of securities transactions by a broker. This section also is not intended to apply to the audit of transactions arising from financial interests in partnerships, corporations, and joint ventures, such as working interests in oil and gas ventures, when proprietary interests are accounted for and reported to interest holders. [As amended, effective December 1999, by Statement on Auditing Standards No. 88. Revised, April 2002, to reflect conforming changes necessary due to the issuance of Statement on Auditing Standards No. 94.]

---

[2] In this section, a service organization's controls that may be relevant to a user organization's internal control as it relates to an audit of financial statements will be referred to as a service organization's *controls*.

.04 This section is organized into the following sections:

a. The user auditor's consideration of the effect of the service organization on the user organization's internal control and the availability of evidence to—

- Obtain the necessary understanding of the user organization's internal control to plan the audit

- Assess control risk at the user organization

- Perform substantive procedures

b. Considerations in using a service auditor's report

c. Responsibilities of service auditors

# The User Auditor's Consideration of the Effect of the Service Organization on the User Organization's Internal Control and the Availability of Audit Evidence

.05 The user auditor should consider the discussion in paragraphs .06 through .21 when planning and performing the audit of an entity that uses a service organization to process its transactions.

## The Effect of Use of a Service Organization on a User Organization's Internal Control

.06 When a user organization uses a service organization, transactions that affect the user organization's financial statements are subjected to controls that are, at least in part, physically and operationally separate from the user organization. The significance of the controls of the service organization to those of the user organization depends on the nature of the services provided by the service organization, primarily the nature and materiality of the transactions it processes for the user organization and the degree of interaction between its activities and those of the user organization. To illustrate how the degree of interaction affects user organization controls, when the user organization initiates transactions and the service organization executes and does the accounting processing of those transactions, there is a high degree of interaction between the activities at the user organization and those at the service organization. In these circumstances, it may be practicable for the user organization to implement effective controls for those transactions. However, when the service organization initiates, executes, and does the accounting processing of the user organization's transactions, there is a lower degree of interaction and it may not be practicable for the user organization to implement effective controls for those transactions. [As amended, effective December 1999, by Statement on Auditing Standards No. 88.]

## Planning the Audit

.07 Section 319, *Consideration of Internal Control in a Financial Statement Audit*, states that an auditor should obtain an understanding of each of the five components of the entity's internal control sufficient to plan the audit. This understanding may encompass controls placed in operation by the entity and by service organizations whose services are part of the entity's information system. In planning the audit, such knowledge should be used to—

- Identify types of potential misstatements.
- Consider factors that affect the risk of material misstatement.
- Design tests of controls, when applicable. Paragraphs 65 through 69 of SAS No. 55 discuss factors the auditor considers in determining whether to perform tests of controls
- Design substantive tests.

[As amended, effective for service auditor's reports covering descriptions as of or after January 1, 1997, by Statement on Auditing Standards No. 78. As amended, effective December 1999, by Statement on Auditing Standards No. 88. Revised, May 2001, to reflect conforming changes necessary due to the issuance of Statement on Auditing Standards No. 94.]

[.08] [Paragraph deleted by the issuance of Statement on Auditing Standards No. 88, December 1999.]

.09 Information about the nature of the services provided by a service organization that are part of the user organization's information system and the service organization's controls over those services may be available from a wide variety of sources, such as user manuals, system overviews, technical manuals, the contract between the user organization and the service organization, and reports by service auditors, internal auditors, or regulatory authorities on the service organization's controls. If the services and the service organization's controls over those services are highly standardized, information obtained through the user auditor's prior experience with the service organization may be helpful in planning the audit. [As amended, effective December 1999, by Statement on Auditing Standards No. 88.]

.10 After considering the available information, the user auditor may conclude that he or she has the means to obtain a sufficient understanding of internal control to plan the audit. If the user auditor concludes that information is not available to obtain a sufficient understanding to plan the audit, he or she may consider contacting the service organization, through the user organization, to obtain specific information or request that a service auditor be engaged to perform procedures that will supply the necessary information, or the user auditor may visit the service organization and perform such procedures. If the user auditor is unable to obtain sufficient evidence to achieve his or her audit objectives, the user auditor should qualify his or her opinion or disclaim an opinion on the financial statements because of a scope limitation. [As amended, effective December 1999, by Statement on Auditing Standards No. 88.]

## Assessing Control Risk at the User Organization

.11 The user auditor uses his or her understanding of the internal control to assess control risk for the assertions embodied in the account balances and classes of transactions, including those that are affected by the activities of the service organization. In doing so, the user auditor may identify certain user organization controls that, if effective, would permit the user auditor to assess control risk below the maximum for particular assertions. Such controls may be applied at either the user organization or the service organization. The user auditor may conclude that it would be efficient to obtain evidential matter about the operating effectiveness of controls to provide a basis for assessing control risk below the maximum. [Revised, April 2002, to reflect conforming changes necessary due to the issuance of Statement on Auditing Standards No. 94.]

**.12** A service auditor's report on controls placed in operation at the service organization should be helpful in providing a sufficient understanding to plan the audit of the user organization. Such a report, however, is not intended to provide any evidence of the operating effectiveness of the relevant controls that would allow the user auditor to reduce the assessed level of control risk below the maximum. Such evidential matter should be derived from one or more of the following:

    *a.* Tests of the user organization's controls over the activities of the service organization (for example, the user auditor may test the user organization's independent reperformance of selected items processed by a service organization or test the user organization's reconciliation of output reports with source documents)

    *b.* A service auditor's report on controls placed in operation and tests of operating effectiveness, or a report on the application of agreed-upon procedures that describes relevant tests of controls

    *c.* Appropriate tests of controls performed by the user auditor at the service organization

**.13** The user organization may establish effective controls over the service organization's activities that may be tested and that may enable the user auditor to reduce the assessed level of control risk below the maximum for some or all of the related assertions. If a user organization, for example, uses a service organization to process its payroll transactions, the user organization may establish controls over the submission and receipt of payroll information that could prevent or detect material misstatements. The user organization might reperform the service organization's payroll calculations on a test basis. In this situation, the user auditor may perform tests of the user organization's controls over payroll processing that would provide a basis for assessing control risk below the maximum for the assertions related to payroll transactions. Alternatively, the user auditor may decide to assess control risk at the maximum level because he or she believes controls are unlikely to pertain to an assertion, are unlikely to be effective, or because he or she believes obtaining evidence about the operating effectiveness of the service organization's controls, such as those over changes in payroll programs, would not be efficient. [Revised, April 2002, to reflect conforming changes necessary due to the issuance of Statement on Auditing Standards No. 94.]

**.14** The user auditor may find that controls relevant to assessing control risk below the maximum for particular assertions are applied only at the service organization. If the user auditor plans to assess control risk below the maximum for those assertions, he or she should evaluate the operating effectiveness of those controls by obtaining a service auditor's report that describes the results of the service auditor's tests of those controls (that is, a report on controls placed in operation and tests of operating effectiveness, or an agreed-upon procedures report)[3] or by performing tests of controls at the service organization.

---

[3] See AT section 201, *Agreed-Upon Procedures Engagements,* for guidance on performing and reporting on agreed-upon procedures engagements. [Footnote added, April 2002, to reflect conforming changes necessary due to the issuance of Statement on Standards for Attestation Engagements No. 10.]

If the user auditor decides to use a service auditor's report, the user auditor should consider the extent of the evidence provided by the report about the effectiveness of controls intended to prevent or detect material misstatements in the particular assertions. The user auditor remains responsible for evaluating the evidence presented by the service auditor and for determining its effect on the assessment of control risk at the user organization.

.15    The user auditor's assessments of control risk regarding assertions about account balances or classes of transactions are based on the combined evidence provided by the service auditor's report and the user auditor's own procedures. In making these assessments, the user auditor should consider the nature, source, and interrelationships among the evidence, as well as the period covered by the tests of controls. The user auditor uses the assessed levels of control risk, as well as his or her understanding of internal control, in determining the nature, timing, and extent of substantive tests for particular assertions.

.16    The guidance in section 319.90 through .99, regarding the auditor's consideration of the sufficiency of evidential matter to support a specific assessed level of control risk is applicable to user auditors considering evidential matter provided by a service auditor's report on controls placed in operation and tests of operating effectiveness. Because the report may be intended to satisfy the needs of several different user auditors, a user auditor should determine whether the specific tests of controls and results in the service auditor's report are relevant to assertions that are significant in the user organization's financial statements. For those tests of controls and results that are relevant, a user auditor should consider whether the nature, timing, and extent of such tests of controls and results provide appropriate evidence about the effectiveness of the controls to support the user auditor's assessed level of control risk. In evaluating these factors, user auditors should also keep in mind that, for certain assumptions, the shorter the period covered by a specific test and the longer the time elapsed since the performance of the test, the less support for control risk reduction the test may provide. [Revised, May 2001, to reflect conforming changes necessary due to the issuance of Statement on Auditing Standards No. 94.]

## Audit Evidence From Substantive Audit Procedures Performed by Service Auditors

.17    Service auditors may be engaged to perform procedures that are substantive in nature for the benefit of user auditors. Such engagements may involve the performance, by the service auditor, of procedures agreed upon by the user organization and its auditor and by the service organization and its auditor. In addition, there may be requirements imposed by governmental authorities or through contractual arrangements whereby service auditors perform designated procedures that are substantive in nature. The results of the application of the required procedures to balances and transactions processed by the service organization may be used by user auditors as part of the evidence necessary to support their opinions.

## Considerations in Using a Service Auditor's Report

.18    In considering whether the service auditor's report is satisfactory for his or her purposes, the user auditor should make inquiries concerning the service auditor's professional reputation. Appropriate sources of information concerning the professional reputation of the service auditor are discussed in section 543, *Part of Audit Performed by Other Independent Auditors*, paragraph .10*a*.

**.19** In considering whether the service auditor's report is sufficient to meet his or her objectives, the user auditor should give consideration to the guidance in section 543.12. If the user auditor believes that the service auditor's report may not be sufficient to meet his or her objectives, the user auditor may supplement his or her understanding of the service auditor's procedures and conclusions by discussing with the service auditor the scope and results of the service auditor's work. Also, if the user auditor believes it is necessary, he or she may contact the service organization, through the user organization, to request that the service auditor perform agreed-upon procedures at the service organization, or the user auditor may perform such procedures.

**.20** When assessing a service organization's controls and how they interact with a user organization's controls, the user auditor may become aware of the existence of reportable conditions. In such circumstances, the user auditor should consider the guidance provided in section 325, *Communication of Internal Control Related Matters Noted in an Audit*.[4]

**.21** The user auditor should not make reference to the report of the service auditor as a basis, in part, for his or her own opinion on the user organization's financial statements. The service auditor's report is used in the audit, but the service auditor is not responsible for examining any portion of the financial statements as of any specific date or for any specified period. Thus, there cannot be a division of responsibility for the audit of the financial statements.

# Responsibilities of Service Auditors

**.22** The service auditor is responsible for the representations in his or her report and for exercising due care in the application of procedures that support those representations. Although a service auditor's engagement differs from an audit of financial statements conducted in accordance with generally accepted auditing standards, it should be performed in accordance with the general standards and with the relevant fieldwork and reporting standards. Although the service auditor should be independent from the service organization, it is not necessary for the service auditor to be independent from each user organization.

**.23** As a result of procedures performed at the service organization, the service auditor may become aware of illegal acts, fraud, or uncorrected errors attributable to the service organization's management or employees that may affect one or more user organizations. The terms *errors*, *fraud*, and *illegal acts* are discussed in section 312, *Audit Risk and Materiality in Conducting an Audit*, and section 317, *Illegal Acts by Clients*; the discussions therein are relevant to this section. When the service auditor becomes aware of such matters, he or she should determine from the appropriate level of management of the service organization whether this information has been communicated appropriately

---

[4] For issuers, PCAOB Release 2004-008 amends paragraph 20 of SAS 70 as follows: The term "reportable conditions" is replaced by the term "significant deficiencies" and the reference to section 325, *Communication of Internal Control Related Matters Noted in an Audit*, is replaced by the reference to section 325, *Communications About Control Deficiencies in An Audit of Financial Statements*. [Footnote added as part of the 2005 conforming changes to this edition of the Guide. This footnote is not included in AU section 324 of AICPA *Professional Standards*.]

to affected user organizations, unless those matters are clearly inconsequential. If the management of the service organization has not communicated the information to affected user organizations and is unwilling to do so, the service auditor should inform the service organization's audit committee or others with equivalent authority or responsibility. If the audit committee does not respond appropriately to the service auditor's communication, the service auditor should consider whether to resign from the engagement. The service auditor may wish to consult with his or her attorney in making this decision.

.24    The type of engagement to be performed and the related report to be prepared should be established by the service organization. However, when circumstances permit, discussions between the service organization and the user organizations are advisable to determine the type of report that will be most suitable for the user organizations' needs. This section provides guidance on the two types of reports that may be issued:

a. *Reports on controls placed in operation*—A service auditor's report on a service organization's description of the controls that may be relevant to a user organization's internal control as it relates to an audit of financial statements, on whether such controls were suitably designed to achieve specified control objectives, and on whether they had been placed in operation as of a specific date. Such reports may be useful in providing a user auditor with an understanding of the controls necessary to plan the audit and to design effective tests of controls and substantive tests at the user organization, but they are not intended to provide the user auditor with a basis for reducing his or her assessments of control risk below the maximum.

b. *Reports on controls placed in operation and tests of operating effectiveness*—A service auditor's report on a service organization's description of the controls that may be relevant to a user organization's internal control as it relates to an audit of financial statements, on whether such controls were suitably designed to achieve specified control objectives, on whether they had been placed in operation as of a specific date, and on whether the controls that were tested were operating with sufficient effectiveness to provide reasonable, but not absolute, assurance that the related control objectives were achieved during the period specified. Such reports may be useful in providing the user auditor with an understanding of the controls necessary to plan the audit and may also provide the user auditor with a basis for reducing his or her assessments of control risk below the maximum.

## Reports on Controls Placed in Operation

.25    The information necessary for a report on controls placed in operation ordinarily is obtained through discussions with appropriate service organization personnel and through reference to various forms of documentation, such as system flowcharts and narratives.

.26    After obtaining a description of the relevant controls, the service auditor should determine whether the description provides sufficient information for user auditors to obtain an understanding of those aspects of the service organization's controls that may be relevant to a user organization's internal control. The description should contain a discussion of the features of the service organization's controls that would have an effect on a user organization's internal control. Such features are relevant when they directly affect the service provided to the user organization. They may include controls within the control environment, risk assessment, control activities, information and communication, and monitoring components of internal control. The control environment may include hiring practices and key areas of authority and responsibility. Risk assessment may include the identification of risks associated with processing specific transactions. Control activities may include policies and procedures over the modification of computer programs and are ordinarily designed to meet specific control objectives. The specific control objectives of the service organization should be set forth in the service organization's description of controls. Information and communication may include ways in which user transactions are initiated and processed. Monitoring may include the involvement of internal auditors. [As amended, effective for service auditor's reports covering descriptions as of or after January 1, 1997, by Statement on Auditing Standards No. 78.]

.27 Evidence of whether controls have been placed in operation is ordinarily obtained through previous experience with the service organization and through procedures such as inquiry of appropriate management, supervisory, and staff personnel; inspection of service organization documents and records; and observation of service organization activities and operations. For the type of report described in paragraph .24a, these procedures need not be supplemented by tests of the operating effectiveness of the service organization's controls.

.28 Although a service auditor's report on controls placed in operation is as of a specified date, the service auditor should inquire about changes in the service organization's controls that may have occurred before the beginning of fieldwork. If the service auditor believes that the changes would be considered significant by user organizations and their auditors, those changes should be included in the description of the service organization's controls. If the service auditor concludes that the changes would be considered significant by user organization's and their auditors and the changes are not included in the description of the service organization's controls, the service auditor should describe the changes in his or her report. Such changes might include—

- Procedural changes made to accommodate provisions of a new FASB Statement of Financial Accounting Standards.
- Major changes in an application to permit on-line processing.
- Procedural changes to eliminate previously identified deficiencies.

Changes that occurred more than twelve months before the date being reported on normally would not be considered significant, because they generally would not affect user auditors' considerations.

.29 A service auditor's report expressing an opinion on a description of controls placed in operation at a service organization should contain—

  a. A specific reference to the applications, services, products, or other aspects of the service organization covered.
  b. A description of the scope and nature of the service auditor's procedures.
  c. Identification of the party specifying the control objectives.
  d. An indication that the purpose of the service auditor's engagement was to obtain reasonable assurance about whether (1) the service organization's description presents fairly, in all material respects,

the aspects of the service organization's controls that may be relevant to a user organization's internal control as it relates to an audit of financial statements, (2) the controls were suitably designed to achieve specified control objectives, and (3) such controls had been placed in operation as of a specific date.

e. A disclaimer of opinion on the operating effectiveness of the controls.

f. The service auditor's opinion on whether the description presents fairly, in all material respects, the relevant aspects of the service organization's controls that had been placed in operation as of a specific date and whether, in the service auditor's opinion, the controls were suitably designed to provide reasonable assurance that the specified control objectives would be achieved if those controls were complied with satisfactorily.

g. A statement of the inherent limitations of the potential effectiveness of controls at the service organization and of the risk of projecting to future periods any evaluation of the description.

h. Identification of the parties for whom the report is intended.

**.30**   If the service auditor believes that the description is inaccurate or insufficiently complete for user auditors, the service auditor's report should so state and should contain sufficient detail to provide user auditors with an appropriate understanding.

**.31**   It may become evident to the service auditor, when considering the service organization's description of controls placed in operation, that the system was designed with the assumption that certain controls would be implemented by the user organization. If the service auditor is aware of the need for such complementary user organization controls, these should be delineated in the description of controls. If the application of controls by user organizations is necessary to achieve the stated control objectives, the service auditor's report should be modified to include the phrase "and user organizations applied the controls contemplated in the design of the Service Organization's controls" following the words "complied with satisfactorily" in the scope and opinion paragraphs.

**.32**   The service auditor should consider conditions that come to his or her attention that, in the service auditor's judgment, represent significant deficiencies in the design or operation of the service organization's controls that preclude the service auditor from obtaining reasonable assurance that specified control objectives would be achieved. The service auditor should also consider whether any other information, irrespective of specified control objectives, has come to his or her attention that causes him or her to conclude (a) that design deficiencies exist that could adversely affect the ability to initiate, record, process, or report financial data to user organizations without error, and (b) that user organizations would not generally be expected to have controls in place to mitigate such design deficiencies. [Revised, April 2002, to reflect conforming changes necessary due to the issuance of Statement on Auditing Standards No. 94.]

**.33**   The description of controls and control objectives required for these reports may be prepared by the service organization. If the service auditor prepares the description of controls and control objectives, the representations in the description remain the responsibility of the service organization.

**.34** For the service auditor to express an opinion on whether the controls were suitably designed to achieve the specified control objectives, it is necessary that—

    *a.* The service organization identify and appropriately describe such control objectives and the relevant controls.

    *b.* The service auditor consider the linkage of the controls to the stated control objectives.

    *c.* The service auditor obtain sufficient evidence to reach an opinion.

**.35** The control objectives may be designated by the service organization or by outside parties such as regulatory authorities, a user group, or others. When the control objectives are not established by outside parties, the service auditor should be satisfied that the control objectives, as set forth by the service organization, are reasonable in the circumstances and consistent with the service organization's contractual obligations.

**.36** The service auditor's report should state whether the controls were suitably designed to achieve the specified control objectives. The report should not state whether they were suitably designed to achieve objectives beyond the specifically identified control objectives.

**.37** The service auditor's opinion on whether the controls were suitably designed to achieve the specified control objectives is not intended to provide evidence of operating effectiveness or to provide the user auditor with a basis for concluding that control risk may be assessed below the maximum.

**.38** The following is a sample report on controls placed in operation at a service organization. The report should have, as an attachment, a description of the service organization's controls that may be relevant to a user organization's internal control as it relates to an audit of financial statements. This report is illustrative only and should be modified as appropriate to suit the circumstances of individual engagements.

To XYZ Service Organization:

We have examined the accompanying description of controls related to the ____ application of XYZ Service Organization. Our examination included procedures to obtain reasonable assurance about whether (1) the accompanying description presents fairly, in all material respects, the aspects of XYZ Service Organization's controls that may be relevant to a user organization's internal control as it relates to an audit of financial statements, (2) the controls included in the description were suitably designed to achieve the control objectives specified in the description, if those controls were complied with satisfactorily,[5] and (3) such controls had been placed in operation as of ____. The control objectives were specified by ____. Our examination was performed in accordance with standards established by the American Institute of Certified

---

[5] If the application of controls by user organizations is necessary to achieve the stated control objectives, the service auditor's report should be modified to include the phrase "and user organizations applied the controls contemplated in the design of XYZ Service Organization's controls" following the words "complied with satisfactorily" in the scope and opinion paragraphs. [Footnote renumbered, April 2002, to reflect conforming changes necessary due to the issuance of Statement on Standards for Attestation Engagements No. 10.]

Public Accountants and included those procedures we considered necessary in the circumstances to obtain a reasonable basis for rendering our opinion.

We did not perform procedures to determine the operating effectiveness of controls for any period. Accordingly, we express no opinion on the operating effectiveness of any aspects of XYZ Service Organization's controls, individually or in the aggregate.

In our opinion, the accompanying description of the aforementioned application presents fairly, in all material respects, the relevant aspects of XYZ Service Organization's controls that had been placed in operation as of ___. Also, in our opinion, the controls, as described, are suitably designed to provide reasonable assurance that the specified control objectives would be achieved if the described controls were complied with satisfactorily.

The description of controls at XYZ Service Organization is as of ____ and any projection of such information to the future is subject to the risk that, because of change, the description may no longer portray the controls in existence. The potential effectiveness of specific controls at the Service Organization is subject to inherent limitations and, accordingly, errors or fraud may occur and not be detected. Furthermore, the projection of any conclusions, based on our findings, to future periods is subject to the risk that changes may alter the validity of such conclusions.

This report is intended solely for use by the management of XYZ Service Organization, its customers, and the independent auditors of its customers ___.

**.39** If the service auditor concludes that the description is inaccurate or insufficiently complete for user auditors, the service auditor should so state in an explanatory paragraph preceding the opinion paragraph. An example of such an explanatory paragraph follows:

The accompanying description states that XYZ Service Organization uses operator identification numbers and passwords to prevent unauthorized access to the system. Based on inquiries of staff personnel and inspections of activities, we determined that such procedures are employed in Applications A and B but are not required to access the system in Applications C and D.

In addition, the first sentence of the opinion paragraph would be modified to read as follows:

In our opinion, except for the matter referred to in the preceding paragraph, the accompanying description of the aforementioned application presents fairly, in all material respects, the relevant aspects of XYZ Service Organization's controls that had been placed in operation as of ___.

**.40** If, after applying the criteria in paragraph .32, the service auditor concludes that there are significant deficiencies in the design or operation of the service organization's controls, the service auditor should report those conditions in an explanatory paragraph preceding the opinion paragraph. An example of an explanatory paragraph describing a significant deficiency in the design or operation of the service organization's controls follows:

> As discussed in the accompanying description, from time to time the Service Organization makes changes in application programs to correct deficiencies or to enhance capabilities. The procedures followed in determining whether to make changes, in designing the changes, and in implementing them do not include review and approval by authorized individuals who are independent from those involved in making the changes. There are also no specified requirements to test such changes or provide test results to an authorized reviewer prior to implementing the changes.

In addition, the second sentence of the opinion paragraph would be modified to read as follows:

> Also in our opinion, except for the deficiency referred to in the preceding paragraph, the controls, as described, are suitably designed to provide reasonable assurance that the specified control objectives would be achieved if the described controls were complied with satisfactorily.

## Reports on Controls Placed in Operation and Tests of Operating Effectiveness

*Paragraphs .41 through .56 repeat some of the information contained in paragraphs .25 through .40 to provide readers with a comprehensive, stand-alone presentation of the relevant considerations for each type of report.*

**.41** The information necessary for a report on controls placed in operation and tests of operating effectiveness ordinarily is obtained through discussions with appropriate service organization personnel, through reference to various forms of documentation, such as system flowcharts and narratives, and through the performance of tests of controls. Evidence of whether controls have been placed in operation is ordinarily obtained through previous experience with the service organization and through procedures such as inquiry of appropriate management, supervisory, and staff personnel; inspection of service organization documents and records; and observation of service organization activities and operations. The service auditor applies tests of controls to determine whether specific controls are operating with sufficient effectiveness to achieve specified control objectives. Section 350, *Audit Sampling*, provides guidance on the application and evaluation of audit sampling in performing tests of controls.

**.42** After obtaining a description of the relevant controls, the service auditor should determine whether the description provides sufficient information for user auditors to obtain an understanding of those aspects of the service organization's controls that may be relevant to a user organization's internal control. The description should contain a discussion of the features of the service organization's controls that would have an effect on a user organization's internal control. Such features are relevant when they directly affect the service provided to the user organization. They may include controls within the control environment, risk assessment, control activities, information and communication, and monitoring components of internal control. The control environment

**AAG-SRV APP F**

may include hiring practices and key areas of authority and responsibility. Risk assessment may include the identification of risks associated with processing specific transactions. Control activities may include policies and procedures over the modification of computer programs and are ordinarily designed to meet specific control objectives. The specific control objectives of the service organization should be set forth in the service organization's description of controls. Information and communication may include ways in which user transactions are initiated and processed. Monitoring may include the involvement of internal auditors. [As amended, effective for service auditor's reports covering descriptions as of or after January 1, 1997, by Statement on Auditing Standards No. 78.]

**.43** The service auditor should inquire about changes in the service organization's controls that may have occurred before the beginning of fieldwork. If the service auditor believes the changes would be considered significant by user organizations and their auditors, those changes should be included in the description of the service organization's controls. If the service auditor concludes that the changes would be considered significant by user organizations and their auditors and the changes are not included in the description of the service organization's controls, the service auditor should describe the changes in his or her report. Such changes might include—

- Procedural changes made to accommodate provisions of a new FASB Statement of Financial Accounting Standards.
- Major changes in an application to permit on-line processing.
- Procedural changes to eliminate previously identified deficiencies.

Changes that occurred more than twelve months before the date being reported on normally would not be considered significant, because they generally would not affect user auditors' considerations.

**.44** A service auditor's report expressing an opinion on a description of controls placed in operation at a service organization and tests of operating effectiveness should contain—

*a.* A specific reference to the applications, services, products, or other aspects of the service organization covered.

*b.* A description of the scope and nature of the service auditor's procedures.

*c.* Identification of the party specifying the control objectives.

*d.* An indication that the purpose of the service auditor's engagement was to obtain reasonable assurance about whether (1) the service organization's description presents fairly, in all material respects, the aspects of the service organization's controls that may be relevant to a user organization's internal control as it relates to an audit of financial statements, (2) the controls were suitably designed to achieve specified control objectives, and (3) such controls had been placed in operation as of a specific date.

*e.* The service auditor's opinion on whether the description presents fairly, in all material respects, the relevant aspects of the service organization's controls that had been placed in operation as of a specific date and whether, in the service auditor's opinion, the controls were suitably designed to provide reasonable assurance that the specified control objectives would be achieved if those controls were complied with satisfactorily.

*f.* A reference to a description of tests of specific service organization controls designed to obtain evidence about the operating effectiveness of those controls in achieving specified control objectives. The description should include the controls that were tested, the control objectives the controls were intended to achieve, the tests applied, and the results of the tests. The description should include an indication of the nature, timing, and extent of the tests, as well as sufficient detail to enable user auditors to determine the effect of such tests on user auditors' assessments of control risk. To the extent that the service auditor identified causative factors for exceptions, determined the current status of corrective actions, or obtained other relevant qualitative information about exceptions noted, such information should be provided.

*g.* A statement of the period covered by the service auditor's report on the operating effectiveness of the specific controls tested.

*h.* The service auditor's opinion on whether the controls that were tested were operating with sufficient effectiveness to provide reasonable, but not absolute, assurance that the related control objectives were achieved during the period specified.

*i.* When all of the control objectives listed in the description of controls placed in operation are not covered by tests of operating effectiveness, a statement that the service auditor does not express an opinion on control objectives not listed in the description of tests performed at the service organization.

*j.* A statement that the relative effectiveness and significance of specific service organization controls and their effect on assessments of control risk at user organizations are dependent on their interaction with the controls and other factors present at individual user organizations.

*k.* A statement that the service auditor has performed no procedures to evaluate the effectiveness of controls at individual user organizations.

*l.* A statement of the inherent limitations of the potential effectiveness of controls at the service organization and of the risk of projecting to the future any evaluation of the description or any conclusions about the effectiveness of controls in achieving control objectives.

*m.* Identification of the parties for whom the report is intended.

**.45** If the service auditor believes that the description is inaccurate or insufficiently complete for user auditors, the service auditor's report should so state and should contain sufficient detail to provide user auditors with an appropriate understanding.

**.46** It may become evident to the service auditor, when considering the service organization's description of controls placed in operation, that the system was designed with the assumption that certain controls would be implemented by the user organization. If the service auditor is aware of the need for such complementary user organization controls, these should be delineated in the description of controls. If the application of controls by user organizations is necessary to achieve the stated control objectives, the service auditor's report should be modified to include the phrase "and user organizations applied the controls contemplated in the design of the Service Organization's controls" following the words "complied with satisfactorily" in the scope and opinion paragraphs. Similarly, if the operating effectiveness of controls at the service organization is dependent on the application of controls at user organizations, this should be delineated in the description of tests performed.

**.47** The service auditor should consider conditions that come to his or her attention that, in the service auditor's judgment, represent significant deficiencies in the design or operation of the service organization's controls that preclude the service auditor from obtaining reasonable assurance that specified control objectives would be achieved. The service auditor should also consider whether any other information, irrespective of specified control objectives, has come to his or her attention that causes him or her to conclude (*a*) that design deficiencies exist that could adversely affect the ability to initiate, record, process, or report financial data to user organizations without error, and (*b*) that user organizations would not generally be expected to have controls in place to mitigate such design deficiencies. [Revised, April 2002, to reflect conforming changes necessary due to the issuance of Statement on Auditing Standards No. 94.]

**.48** The description of controls and control objectives required for these reports may be prepared by the service organization. If the service auditor prepares the description of controls and control objectives, the representations in the description remain the responsibility of the service organization.

**.49** For the service auditor to express an opinion on whether the controls were suitably designed to achieve the specified control objectives, it is necessary that—

   *a.* The service organization identify and appropriately describe such control objectives and the relevant controls.

   *b.* The service auditor consider the linkage of the controls to the stated control objectives.

   *c.* The service auditor obtain sufficient evidence to reach an opinion.

**.50** The control objectives may be designated by the service organization or by outside parties such as regulatory authorities, a user group, or others. When the control objectives are not established by outside parties, the service auditor should be satisfied that the control objectives, as set forth by the service organization, are reasonable in the circumstances and consistent with the service organization's contractual obligations.

**.51** The service auditor's report should state whether the controls were suitably designed to achieve the specified control objectives. The report should not state whether they were suitably designed to achieve objectives beyond the specifically identified control objectives.

**.52** The service auditor's opinion on whether the controls were suitably designed to achieve the specified control objectives is not intended to provide evidence of operating effectiveness or to provide the user auditor with a basis for concluding that control risk may be assessed below the maximum. Evidence that may enable the user auditor to conclude that control risk may be assessed below the maximum may be obtained from the results of specific tests of operating effectiveness.

**.53** The management of the service organization specifies whether all or selected applications and control objectives will be covered by the tests of operating effectiveness. The service auditor determines which controls are, in his or her judgment, necessary to achieve the control objectives specified by management. The service auditor then determines the nature, timing, and extent of the tests of controls needed to evaluate operating effectiveness. Testing should be applied to controls in effect throughout the period covered by the report. To be useful to user auditors, the report should ordinarily cover a minimum reporting period of six months.

**.54** The following is a sample report on controls placed in operation at a service organization and tests of operating effectiveness. It should be assumed that the report has two attachments: (*a*) a description of the service organization's controls that may be relevant to a user organization's internal control as it relates to an audit of financial statements and (*b*) a description of controls for which tests of operating effectiveness were performed, the control objectives the controls were intended to achieve, the tests applied, and the results of those tests. This report is illustrative only and should be modified as appropriate to suit the circumstances of individual engagements.

To XYZ Service Organization:

We have examined the accompanying description of controls related to the ____ application of XYZ Service Organization. Our examination included procedures to obtain reasonable assurance about whether (1) the accompanying description presents fairly, in all material respects, the aspects of XYZ Service Organization's controls that may be relevant to a user organization's internal control as it relates to an audit of financial statements, (2) the controls included in the description were suitably designed to achieve the control objectives specified in the description, if those controls were complied with satisfactorily,[6] and (3) such controls had been placed in operation as of ____. The control objectives were specified by ____. Our examination was performed in accordance with standards established by the American Institute of Certified Public Accountants and included those procedures we considered necessary in the circumstances to obtain a reasonable basis for rendering our opinion.

In our opinion, the accompanying description of the aforementioned application presents fairly, in all material respects, the relevant aspects of XYZ Service Organization's controls that had been placed in operation as of __. Also, in our opinion, the controls, as described, are suitably designed to provide reasonable assurance that the specified control objectives would be achieved if the described controls were complied with satisfactorily.

---

[6] If the application of controls by user organizations is necessary to achieve the stated control objectives, the service auditor's report should be modified to include the phrase "and user organizations applied the controls contemplated in the design of XYZ Service Organization's controls" following the words "complied with satisfactorily" in the scope and opinion paragraphs. [Footnote renumbered, April 2002, to reflect conforming changes necessary due to the issuance of Statement on Standards for Attestation Engagements No. 10.]

In addition to the procedures we considered necessary to render our opinion as expressed in the previous paragraph, we applied tests to specific controls, listed in Schedule X, to obtain evidence about their effectiveness in meeting the control objectives, described in Schedule X, during the period from to ___. The specific controls and the nature, timing, extent, and results of the tests are listed in Schedule X. This information has been provided to user organizations of XYZ Service Organization and to their auditors to be taken into consideration, along with information about the internal control at user organizations, when making assessments of control risk for user organizations. In our opinion the controls that were tested, as described in Schedule X, were operating with sufficient effectiveness to provide reasonable, but not absolute, assurance that the control objectives specified in Schedule X were achieved during the period from ___ to ___. [However, the scope of our engagement did not include tests to determine whether control objectives not listed in Schedule X were achieved; accordingly, we express no opinion on the achievement of control objectives not included in Schedule X.][7]

The relative effectiveness and significance of specific controls at XYZ Service Organization and their effect on assessments of control risk at user organizations are dependent on their interaction with the controls and other factors present at individual user organizations. We have performed no procedures to evaluate the effectiveness of controls at individual user organizations.

The description of controls at XYZ Service Organization is as of ___, and information about tests of the operating effectiveness of specific controls covers the period from ___ to ___. Any projection of such information to the future is subject to the risk that, because of change, the description may no longer portray the controls in existence. The potential effectiveness of specific controls at the Service Organization is subject to inherent limitations and, accordingly, errors or fraud may occur and not be detected. Furthermore, the projection of any conclusions, based on our findings, to future periods is subject to the risk that changes may alter the validity of such conclusions.

This report is intended solely for use by the management of XYZ Service Organization, its customers, and the independent auditors of its customers.

.55    If the service auditor concludes that the description is inaccurate or insufficiently complete for user auditors, the service auditor should so state

---

[7] This sentence should be added when all of the control objectives listed in the description of controls placed in operation are not covered by the tests of operating effectiveness. This sentence would be omitted when all of the control objectives listed in the description of controls placed in operation are included in the tests of operating effectiveness. [Footnote renumbered, April 2002, to reflect conforming changes necessary due to the issuance of Statement on Standards for Attestation Engagements No. 10.]

in an explanatory paragraph preceding the opinion paragraph. An example of such an explanatory paragraph follows:

> The accompanying description states that XYZ Service Organization uses operator identification numbers and passwords to prevent unauthorized access to the system. Based on inquiries of staff personnel and inspection of activities, we determined that such procedures are employed in Applications A and B but are not required to access the system in Applications C and D.

In addition, the first sentence of the opinion paragraph would be modified to read as follows:

> In our opinion, except for the matter referred to in the preceding paragraph, the accompanying description of the aforementioned application presents fairly, in all material respects, the relevant aspects of XYZ Service Organization's controls that had been placed in operation as of ___.

**.56** If, after applying the criteria in paragraph .47, the service auditor concludes that there are significant deficiencies in the design or operation of the service organization's controls, the service auditor should report those conditions in an explanatory paragraph preceding the opinion paragraph. An example of an explanatory paragraph describing a significant deficiency in the design or operation of the service organization's controls follows:

> As discussed in the accompanying description, from time to time the Service Organization makes changes in application programs to correct deficiencies or to enhance capabilities. The procedures followed in determining whether to make changes, in designing the changes, and in implementing them do not include review and approval by authorized individuals who are independent from those involved in making the changes. There are also no specified requirements to test such changes or provide test results to an authorized reviewer prior to implementing the changes.

In addition, the second sentence of the opinion paragraph would be modified to read as follows:

> Also in our opinion, except for the deficiency referred to in the preceding paragraph, the controls, as described, are suitably designed to provide reasonable assurance that the related control objectives would be achieved if the described controls were complied with satisfactorily.

## Responsibilities of Service Organizations and Service Auditors With Respect to Subsequent Events

**.57** Changes in a service organization's controls that could affect user organizations' information systems may occur subsequent to the period covered by the service auditor's report but before the date of the service auditor's report. These occurrences are referred to as subsequent events. A service auditor should consider information about two types of subsequent events that come to his or her attention. [Paragraph added, effective for reports issued on or after January 1, 2003, by Statement on Auditing Standards No. 98.]

**AAG-SRV APP F**

**.58** The first type consists of events that provide additional information about conditions that existed during the period covered by the service auditor's report. This information should be used by the service auditor in determining whether controls at the service organization that could affect user organizations' information systems were placed in operation, suitably designed, and, if applicable, operating effectively during the period covered by the engagement. [Paragraph added, effective for reports issued on or after January 1, 2003, by Statement on Auditing Standards No. 98.]

**.59** The second type consists of those events that provide information about conditions that arose subsequent to the period covered by the service auditor's report that are of such a nature and significance that their disclosure is necessary to prevent users from being misled. This type of information ordinarily will not affect the service auditor's report if the information is adequately disclosed by management in a section of the report containing "Other Information Provided by the Service Organization." If this information is not disclosed by the service organization, the service auditor should disclose it in a section of the report containing "Other Information Provided by the Service Auditor" and/or in the service auditor's report. [Paragraph added, effective for reports issued on or after January 1, 2003, by Statement on Auditing Standards No. 98.]

**.60** Although a service auditor has no responsibility to detect subsequent events, the service auditor should inquire of management as to whether it is aware of any subsequent events through the date of the service auditor's report that would have a significant effect on user organizations. In addition, a service auditor should obtain a representation from management regarding subsequent events. [Paragraph added, effective for reports issued on or after January 1, 2003, by Statement on Auditing Standards No. 98.]

## Written Representations of the Service Organization's Management

**.61** Regardless of the type of report issued, the service auditor should obtain written representations from the service organization's management that—

- Acknowledge management's responsibility for establishing and maintaining appropriate controls relating to the processing of transactions for user organizations.
- Acknowledge the appropriateness of the specified control objectives.
- State that the description of controls presents fairly, in all material respects, the aspects of the service organization's controls that may be relevant to a user organization's internal control.
- State that the controls, as described, had been placed in operation as of a specific date.
- State that management believes its controls were suitably designed to achieve the specified control objectives.
- State that management has disclosed to the service auditor any significant changes in controls that have occurred since the service organization's last examination.
- State that management has disclosed to the service auditor any illegal acts, fraud, or uncorrected errors attributable to the service

organization's management or employees that may affect one or more user organizations.

- State that management has disclosed to the service auditor all design deficiencies in controls of which it is aware, including those for which management believes the cost of corrective action may exceed the benefits.
- State that management has disclosed to the service auditor any subsequent events that would have a significant effect on user organizations.

If the scope of the work includes tests of operating effectiveness, the service auditor should obtain a written representation from the service organization's management stating that management has disclosed to the service auditor all instances, of which it is aware, when controls have not operated with sufficient effectiveness to achieve the specified control objectives. [Paragraph renumbered and amended, effective for reports issued on or after January 1, 2003, by Statement on Auditing Standards No. 98.]

## Reporting on Substantive Procedures

**.62** The service auditor may be requested to apply substantive procedures to user transactions or assets at the service organization. In such circumstances, the service auditor may make specific reference in his or her report to having carried out the designated procedures or may provide a separate report in accordance with AT section 201, *Agreed-Upon Procedures Engagements*. Either form of reporting should include a description of the nature, timing, extent, and results of the procedures in sufficient detail to be useful to user auditors in deciding whether to use the results as evidence to support their opinions. [Revised, January 2001, to reflect conforming changes necessary due to the issuance of Statement on Standards for Attestation Engagements No. 10. Paragraph renumbered by the issuance of Statement on Auditing Standards No. 98, September 2002.]

## Effective Date

**.63** This section is effective for service auditors' reports dated after March 31, 1993. Earlier application of this section is encouraged. [Paragraph renumbered by issuance of Statement on Auditing Standards No. 98, September 2002.]

# Appendix G

# *AU Section 9324: Service Organizations: Auditing Interpretations of Section 324*

## 1. Describing Tests of Operating Effectiveness and the Results of Such Tests

.01 *Question*—Paragraph .44*f* of section 324, *Service Organizations*, specifies the elements that should be included in a description of tests of operating effectiveness, which is part of a report on controls placed in operation and tests of operating effectiveness. Section 324.44*f* states:

> "...The description should include the controls that were tested, the control objectives the controls were intended to achieve, the tests applied and the results of the tests. The description should include an indication of the nature, timing, and extent of the tests, as well as sufficient detail to enable user auditors to determine the effect of such tests on user auditors' assessments of control risk. To the extent that the service auditor identified causative factors for exceptions, determined the current status of corrective actions, or obtained other relevant qualitative information about exceptions noted, such information should be provided."

When a service auditor performs an engagement that includes tests of operating effectiveness, what information and how much detail should be included in the description of the "tests applied" and the "results of the tests"?

.02 *Interpretation*—In all cases, for each control objective tested, the description of tests of operating effectiveness should include all of the elements listed in section 324.44f, whether or not the service auditor concludes that the control objective has been achieved. The description should provide sufficient information to enable user auditors to assess control risk for financial statement assertions affected by the service organization. The description need not be a duplication of the service auditor's detailed audit program, which in some cases would make the report too voluminous for user auditors and would provide more than the required level of detail.

.03 In describing the nature, timing, and extent of the tests applied, the service auditor also should indicate whether the items tested represent a sample or all of the items in the population, but need not indicate the size of the population. In describing the results of the tests, the service auditor should include exceptions and other information that in the service auditor's judgment could be relevant to user auditors. Such exceptions and other information should be included for each control objective, whether or not the service auditor concludes that the control objective has been achieved. When exceptions that could be relevant to user auditors are noted, the description also should include the following information:

- The size of the sample, when sampling has been used
- The number of exceptions noted
- The nature of the exceptions

If no exceptions or other information that could be relevant to user auditors are identified by the tests, the service auditor should indicate that finding (for example, "No relevant exceptions noted").

[Issue Date: April, 1995.]

## 2. Service Organizations That Use the Services of Other Service Organizations (Subservice Organizations)

**.04** *Question*—A service organization may use the services of another service organization, such as a bank trust department that uses an independent computer processing service organization to perform its data processing. In this situation, the bank trust department is a service organization and the computer processing service organization is considered a subservice organization. How are a user auditor's and a service auditor's procedures affected when a service organization uses a subservice organization?

**.05** *Interpretation*—When a service organization uses a subservice organization, the user auditor should determine whether the processing performed by the subservice organization affects assertions in the user organization's financial statements and whether those assertions are significant to the user organization's financial statements. To plan the audit and assess control risk, a user auditor may need to consider the controls at both the service organization and the subservice organization. Paragraphs .06 through .17 of section 324, *Service Organizations*, provide guidance to user auditors on considering the effect of a service organization on a user organization's internal control. Although section 324.06-.17 do not specifically refer to subservice organizations, when a subservice organization provides services to a service organization, the guidance in these paragraphs should be interpreted to include the subservice organization. For example, in situations where subservice organizations are used, the interaction between the user organization and the service organization described in section 324.06 would be expanded to include the interaction between the user organization, the service organization and the subservice organization.

**.06** Similarly, a service auditor engaged to examine the controls of a service organization and issue a service auditor's report may need to consider functions performed by the subservice organization and the effect of the subservice organization's controls on the service organization.

**.07** The degree of interaction and the nature and materiality of the transactions processed by the service organization and the subservice organization are the most important factors to consider in determining the significance of the subservice organization's controls to the user organization's internal control. Section 324.11-.16 describes how a user auditor's assessment of control risk is affected when a user organization uses a service organization. When a subservice organization is involved, the user auditor may need to consider activities at both the service organization and the subservice organization in applying the guidance in these paragraphs.

**.08** *Question*—How does a user auditor obtain information about controls at a subservice organization?

**.09** *Interpretation*—If a user auditor concludes that he or she needs information about the subservice organization to plan the audit or to assess control risk, the user auditor (*a*) may contact the service organization through the user organization and may contact the subservice organization either through the user organization or the service organization to obtain specific information or (*b*) may request that a service auditor be engaged to perform procedures that will supply the necessary information. Alternatively, the user auditor may visit the service organization or subservice organization and perform such procedures.

**.10** *Question*—When a service organization uses a subservice organization, what information about the subservice organization should be included in the service organization's description of controls?

**.11** *Interpretation*—A service organization's description of controls should include a description of the functions and nature of the processing performed by the subservice organization in sufficient detail for user auditors to understand the significance of the subservice organization's functions to the processing of the user organizations' transactions. Ordinarily, disclosure of the identity of the subservice organization is not required. However, if the service organization determines that the identity of the subservice organization would be relevant to user organizations, the name of the subservice organization may be included in the description. The purpose of the description of the functions and nature of the processing performed by the subservice organization is to alert user organizations and their auditors to the fact that another entity (that is, the subservice organization) is involved in the processing of the user organizations' transactions and to summarize the functions the subservice organization performs.

**.12** When a subservice organization performs services for a service organization, there are two alternative methods of presenting the description of controls. The service organization determines which method will be used.

  a. *The Carve-Out Method*—The subservice organization's relevant control objectives and controls are excluded from the description and from the scope of the service auditor's engagement. The service organization states in the description that the subservice organization's control objectives and related controls are omitted from the description and that the control objectives in the report include only the objectives the service organization's controls are intended to achieve.

  b. *The Inclusive Method*—The subservice organization's relevant controls are included in the description and in the scope of the engagement. The description should clearly differentiate between controls of the service organization and controls of the subservice organization. The set of control objectives includes all of the objectives a user auditor would expect both the service organization and the subservice organization to achieve. To accomplish this, the service organization should coordinate the preparation and presentation of the description of controls with the subservice organization.

In either method, the service organization includes in its description of controls a description of the functions and nature of the processing performed by the subservice organization, as set forth in paragraph .11.

**.13** If the functions and processing performed by the subservice organization are significant to the processing of user organization transactions, and the service organization does not disclose the existence of the subservice organization and the functions it performs, the service auditor may need to issue a qualified or adverse opinion as to the fairness of the presentation of the description of controls.

**.14** *Question*—How is the service auditor's report affected by the method of presentation selected?

**.15** *Interpretation*—If the service organization has adopted the carve-out method, the service auditor should modify the scope paragraph of the service auditor's report to briefly summarize the functions and nature of the processing performed by the subservice organization. This summary ordinarily would be briefer than the information provided by the service organization in its description of the functions and nature of the processing performed by the subservice organization. The service auditor should include a statement in the scope paragraph of the service auditor's report indicating that the description of controls includes only the control objectives and related controls of the service organization; accordingly, the service auditor's examination does not extend to controls at the subservice organization.

**.16** An example of the scope paragraph of a service auditor's report using the carve-out method is presented below. Additional or modified report language is shown in ***boldface italics***.

## Sample Scope Paragraph of a Service Auditor's Report Using the Carve-Out Method

Independent Service Auditor's Report

To the Board of Directors of Example Trust Company:

We have examined the accompanying description of the controls of Example Trust Company applicable to the processing of transactions for users of the Institutional Trust Division. Our examination included procedures to obtain reasonable assurance about whether (1) the accompanying description presents fairly, in all material respects, the aspects of Example Trust Company's controls that may be relevant to a user organization's internal control as it relates to an audit of financial statements; (2) the controls included in the description were suitably designed to achieve the control objectives specified in the description, if those controls were complied with satisfactorily, and user organizations applied the controls contemplated in the design of Example Trust Company's controls; and (3) such controls had been placed in operation as of June 30, 20XX. ***Example Trust Company uses a computer processing service organization for all of its computerized application processing. The accompanying description includes only those control objectives and related controls of Example Trust Company and does not include control objectives and related controls of the computer processing service organization. Our examination did not extend to controls of the computer processing service organization.*** The control objectives were specified by the management of Example Trust

Company. Our examination was performed in accordance with standards established by the American Institute of Certified Public Accountants and included those procedures we considered necessary in the circumstances to obtain a reasonable basis for rendering our opinion.

[The remainder of the report is the same as the standard service auditor's report illustrated in section 324.38 and .54.]

**.17** If the service organization has used the inclusive method, the service auditor should perform procedures comparable to those described in section 324.12. Such procedures may include performing tests of the service organization's controls over the activities of the subservice organization or performing procedures at the subservice organization. If the service auditor will be performing procedures at the subservice organization, the service organization should arrange for such procedures. The service auditor should recognize that the subservice organization generally is not the client for the engagement. Accordingly, in these circumstances the service auditor should determine whether it will be possible to obtain the required evidence to support the portion of the opinion covering the subservice organization and whether it will be possible to obtain an appropriate letter of representations regarding the subservice organization's controls.

**.18** An example of a service auditor's report using the inclusive method is presented below. Additional or modified report language is shown in ***boldface italics***.

## Sample Service Auditor's Report Using the Inclusive Method

Independent Service Auditor's Report

To the Board of Directors of Example Trust Company:

We have examined the accompanying description of the controls of Example Trust Company ***and Computer Processing Service Organization, an independent service organization that provides computer processing services to Example Trust Company,*** applicable to the processing of transactions for users of the Institutional Trust Division. Our examination included procedures to obtain reasonable assurance about whether (1) the accompanying description presents fairly, in all material respects, the aspects of Example Trust Company's ***and Computer Processing Service Organization's*** controls that may be relevant to a user organization's internal control as it relates to an audit of financial statements; (2) the controls included in the description were suitably designed to achieve the control objectives specified in the description, if those controls were complied with satisfactorily, and user organizations applied the controls contemplated in the design of Example Trust Company's controls; and (3) the controls had been placed in operation as of June 30, 20XX. The control objectives were specified by the management of Example Trust Company. Our examination was performed in accordance with standards established by the American Institute of Certified Public Accountants and included those procedures we considered necessary in the circumstances to obtain a reasonable basis for rendering our opinion.

In our opinion, the accompanying description of the aforementioned controls presents fairly, in all material respects, the relevant aspects of Example Trust Company's *and Computer Processing Service Organization's* controls that had been placed in operation as of June 30, 20XX. Also, in our opinion, the controls, as described, are suitably designed to provide reasonable assurance that the specified control objectives would be achieved if the described controls were complied with satisfactorily and user organizations applied the controls contemplated in the design of Example Trust Company's controls.

In addition to the procedures we considered necessary to render our opinion as expressed in the previous paragraph, we applied tests to specific controls, listed in Schedule X to obtain evidence about their effectiveness in meeting the control objectives, described in Schedule X, during the period from January 1, 20XX, to June 30, 20XX. The specific controls and the nature, timing, extent, and results of the tests are listed in Schedule X. This information has been provided to user organizations of Example Trust Company and to their auditors to be taken into consideration, along with information about internal control at user organizations, when making assessments of control risk for user organizations. In our opinion the controls that were tested, as described in Schedule X, were operating with sufficient effectiveness to provide reasonable, but not absolute, assurance that the control objectives specified in Schedule X were achieved during the period from January 1, 20XX, to June 30, 20XX.

The relative effectiveness and significance of specific controls at Example Trust Company *and Computer Processing Service Organization*, and their effect on assessments of control risk at user organizations are dependent on their interaction with the controls and other factors present at individual user organizations. We have performed no procedures to evaluate the effectiveness of controls at individual user organizations.

The description of controls at Example Trust Company *and Computer Processing Service Organization* is as of June 30, 20XX, and information about tests of the operating effectiveness of specific controls covers the period from January 1, 20XX, to June 30, 20XX. Any projection of such information to the future is subject to the risk that, because of change, the description may no longer portray the controls in existence. The potential effectiveness of specific controls at the Service Organization *and Computer Processing Service Organization* is subject to inherent limitations and, accordingly, errors or fraud may occur and not be detected. Furthermore, the projection of any conclusions, based on our findings, to future periods is subject to the risk that changes may alter the validity of such conclusions.[1]

This report is intended solely for use by the management of Example Trust Company, its users, and the independent auditors of its users.

July 10, 20XX

[Issue Date: April, 1995; Revised: February, 1997; Revised: April, 2002.]

## [3.] Responsibilities of Service Organizations and Service Auditors With Respect to Information About the Year 2000 Issue in a Service Organization's Description of Controls

[.19-.34] [Withdrawn July, 2000 by the Audit Issues Task Force.]

## 4. Responsibilities of Service Organizations and Service Auditors With Respect to Forward-Looking Information in a Service Organization's Description of Controls

**.35** *Question*—Section 324.32 requires a service auditor to consider "whether any other information, irrespective of specified control objectives, has come to his or her attention that causes him or her to conclude (*a*) that design deficiencies exist that could adversely affect the ability to record, process, or report financial data to user organizations without error, and (*b*) that user organizations would not generally be expected to have controls in place to mitigate such design deficiencies." A service auditor performing a service auditor's engagement may become aware that a service organization, whose system is correctly processing data during the period covered by the service auditor's examination, has not performed contingency planning or made adequate provision for disaster recovery, and may not be able to retrieve or process data in future periods. Does section 324.32 require a service auditor to identify, in his or her report, design deficiencies that do not affect processing during the period covered by the service auditor's examination but may represent potential problems in future periods?

**.36** *Interpretation*—No. Section 324.32 addresses design deficiencies that could adversely affect processing *during the period covered by the service auditor's examination*. Section 324.32 does not apply to design deficiencies that potentially could affect processing *in future periods*. If the computer programs are correctly processing data during the period covered by the service auditor's examination, and such design deficiencies currently do not affect user organizations' abilities to record, process, or report financial data, the service auditor would not be required to report such design deficiencies in his or her report, based on the requirements in section 324.32. However, if a service auditor becomes aware of design deficiencies at the service organization that could potentially affect the processing of user organizations' transactions in future periods, the service auditor, in his or her judgment, may choose to communicate this information to the service organization's management and advise management to

---

[1] This sentence has been expanded to describe the risks of projecting any evaluation of the controls to future periods because of the failure to make needed changes to a system or controls, as provided for in Auditing Interpretation No. 5, "Statements About the Risk of Projecting Evaluations of the Effectiveness of Controls to Future Periods" (paragraphs .38–.40).

disclose this information and its plans for correcting the design deficiencies in a section of the service auditor's document titled "Other Information Provided by the Service Organization."[2]

**.37** If the service organization includes information about the design deficiencies in the section of the document titled "Other Information Provided by the Service Organization," the service auditor should read the information and consider applying by analogy the guidance in section 550, *Other Information in Documents Containing Audited Financial Statements.* In addition, the service auditor should include a paragraph in his or her report disclaiming an opinion on the information provided by the service organization. The following is an example of such a paragraph.

> The information in section 4 describing XYZ Service Organization's plans to modify its disaster recovery plan is presented by the Service Organization to provide additional information and is not a part of the Service Organization's description of controls that may be relevant to a user organization's internal control. Such information has not been subjected to the procedures applied in the examination of the description of the controls applicable to the processing of transactions for user organizations and, accordingly, we express no opinion on it.

A service auditor also may consider communicating information about the design deficiencies in the section of the service auditor's document titled "Other Information Provided by the Service Auditor."

[Issue Date: February, 2002.]

## 5. Statements About the Risk of Projecting Evaluations of the Effectiveness of Controls to Future Periods

**.38** *Question*—Section 324.29g and .44l state that a service auditor's report should contain a statement of the inherent limitations of the potential effectiveness of controls at the service organization and of the risk of projecting to future periods any evaluation of the description. Section 324.44l goes on to state that the report also should refer to the risk of projecting to the future "any conclusions about the effectiveness of controls in achieving control objectives." The sample service auditor's reports in section 324.38 and .54 include illustrative paragraphs that illustrate this caveat. The following excerpt is from section 324.54:

> The description of controls at XYZ Service Organization is as of_____, and information about tests of the operating effectiveness of specific controls covers the period from _____

---

[2] Chapter 2 of the AICPA Audit Guide *Service Organizations: Applying SAS No. 70, as Amended*, proposes four sections of a service auditor's document.
1. Independent service auditor's report (the letter from the service auditor expressing his or her opinion)
2. Service organization's description of controls
3. Information provided by the independent service auditor (This section generally contains a description of the service auditor's tests of operating effectiveness and the results of those tests.)
4. Other information provided by the service organization

to _____. Any projection of such information to the future is subject to the risk that, because of change, the description may no longer portray the controls in existence. The potential effectiveness of specific controls at the Service Organization is subject to inherent limitations and, accordingly, errors or fraud may occur and not be detected. Furthermore, the projection of any conclusions, based on our findings, to future periods is subject to the risk that changes may alter the validity of such conclusions.

The validity of projections to the future about the effectiveness of controls may be affected by changes made to the system and the controls, and also by the failure to make needed changes, for example, changes to accommodate new processing requirements. May a service auditor's report be expanded to describe the risk of projecting to the future conclusions about the effectiveness of controls?

**.39** *Interpretation*—The sample reports in section 324.38 and .54 may be expanded to describe this risk. The first and second sentences of the illustrative paragraph above address the potential effect of change on the description of controls as of a specified date; accordingly, they do not require modification because new processing requirements would not affect the description as of the specified date. However, the last sentence in the sample report paragraph above could be expanded to describe the risk of projecting an evaluation of the controls to future periods because of changes to the system or controls, or the failure to make needed changes to the system or controls.

**.40** Suggested additions to the paragraph in the illustrative service auditor's reports in section 324.38 and .54 are the following (new language is shown in italics.):

The description of controls at XYZ Service Organization is as of _____, and information about tests of the operating effectiveness of specific controls covers the period from _____ to _____. Any projection of such information to the future is subject to the risk that, because of change, the description may no longer portray the controls in existence. The potential effectiveness of specific controls at the Service Organization is subject to inherent limitations and, accordingly, errors or fraud may occur and not be detected. Furthermore, the projection of any conclusions, based on our findings, to future periods is subject to the risk that changes *made to the system or controls, or the failure to make needed changes to the system or controls,* may alter the validity of such conclusions.

[Issue Date: February, 2002.]

## [6.] Responsibilities of Service Organizations and Service Auditors With Respect to Subsequent Events in a Service Auditor's Engagement

**[.41–.42]** [Rescinded September, 2002, by Statement on Auditing Standards No. 98.]

# Appendix H

## Schedule of Changes Made to Service Organizations: Applying SAS No. 70, as Amended

### As of May 2005

Beginning May 2001, all schedules of changes reflect only current year activity to improve clarity.

| Reference | Change |
|---|---|
| Preface | Updated to reflect ASB and PCAOB developments and applicability. Former footnote 1 deleted. |
| Introduction | Paragraphs I-04 and I-05 (and footnotes * and †) added to discuss the issuance of PCAOB standards and conforming amendments. Subsequent paragraphs renumbered. |
| Chapter 1 (title) | Footnote * added to refer readers to the Preface for further information about PCAOB standards. |
| Paragraph 1.03 (footnotes 2 and 3) | Added to reflect the conforming amendments in PCAOB Release 2004-008. Subsequent footnotes renumbered. |
| Paragraph 1.05 (renumbered footnote 4) | Revised to reflect the conforming amendments in PCAOB Release 2004-008. |
| Paragraphs 1.09, 1.14, 1.16, and 1.19 | Footnotes 5, 7, 8, 9, 10, 13, and 14 added to reflect the conforming amendments in PCAOB Release 2004-008. Subsequent footnotes renumbered. |
| Chapter 2 (title) | Footnote * added to refer readers to the Preface for further information about PCAOB standards. |
| Paragraphs 2.11 and 2.18 | Footnotes 1 and 3 added to reflect the conforming amendments in PCAOB Release 2004-008. Subsequent footnotes renumbered. |
| Chapter 3 (title) | Footnote * added to refer readers to the Preface for further information about PCAOB standards. |
| Paragraph 3.02 (footnote 1) | Added to reflect the issuance of PCAOB staff questions and answers. Subsequent footnotes renumbered. |
| Paragraphs 3.13 and 3.15 | Footnotes 3 and 4 added to reflect the conforming amendments in PCAOB Release 2004-008. |
| Chapter 4 (title) | Footnote * added to refer readers to the Preface for further information about PCAOB standards. |

| Reference | Change |
|---|---|
| Paragraph 4.11 (footnote 1) | Added to reflect PCAOB staff questions and answers. |
| Paragraph 4.41 (footnote 2) | Added to reflect the conforming amendments in PCAOB Release 2004-008. Subsequent footnotes renumbered. |
| Paragraphs 4.113, 4.120, and 4.124 | Footnotes 4, 5, and 6 added to reflect the conforming amendments in PCAOB Release 2004-008. |
| Chapter 5 (title) | Footnote * added to refer readers to the Preface for further information about PCAOB standards. |
| Paragraph 5.34 (footnote 6) | Added to reflect the conforming amendments in PCAOB Release 2004-008. |
| Appendix F | Footnote 1 added to paragraph .01 and footnote 4 added to paragraph .20 to reflect the conforming amendments in PCAOB Release 2004-008. Subsequent footnotes renumbered. |

# AICPA RESOURCE: Accounting & Auditing Literature

AICPA's unique online research tool combines the power and speed of the W with comprehensive accounting and auditing standards. *AICPA RESOUR* includes AICPA's and FASB's literature libraries—and includes:

- AICPA Professional Standards
- AICPA Technical Practice Aids
- AICPA's Accounting Trends & Techniques
- AICPA Audit and Accounting Guides
- AICPA Audit Risk Alerts
- FASB Original Pronouncements
- FASB Current Text
- EITF Abstracts
- FASB Implementation Guides
- FASB's Comprehensive Topical Index

Search for pertinent information from both databases by keyword and get results ranked by relevancy. Print out important *AICPA RESOURCE* segme and integrate the literature into your engagements and financial stateme Available from anywhere you have Internet access, this comprehen reference library is packed with the A & A guidance you need—and use- most. Both libraries are updated with the latest standards and conforr changes.

**AICPA+FASB reference libraries, one-year individual online subscrip**
No. ORF-XX
AICPA Member $890.00
Nonmember $1,112.50

**AICPA reference library, one-year individual online subscription**
No. ORS-XX
AICPA Member $395.00
Nonmember $493.75

AICPA RESOURCE also offers over 50 additional subscription options—lo onto www.cpa2biz.com/AICPAresource for details.